THE BIBLE *God's Word or Man's?*

Publishers
WATCHTOWER BIBLE AND TRACT SOCIETY OF NEW YORK, INC.
INTERNATIONAL BIBLE STUDENTS ASSOCIATION
Brooklyn, New York, U.S.A.

First Printing in English:
3,000,000 Copies

Unless otherwise indicated,
Scripture quotations are from the modern-language
New World Translation of the Holy Scriptures—With References,
1984 Edition

The Bible—God's Word or Man's?
English (gm-E)
Made in the United States of America

Contents

Picture Credits

Listed by page

▪ Page 9, Edition Leipzig, Werner Pinkert ▪ Page 13, Courtesy of the British Museum ▪ Page 16, Musei Capitolini ▪ Page 21, Israel Department of Antiquities and Museums; Courtesy of the Shrine of the Book, Israel Museum; B. Samuel and Jeane H. Gottesman Center for Biblical Manuscripts ▪ Page 23, Musei Capitolini ▪ Page 26, The Metropolitan Museum of Art, Bequest of Mrs. F. F. Thompson, 1926 (26.229) ▪ Page 29, Sacro Speco, Subiaco ▪ Page 35, Photo by C.N. ▪ Page 45, Courtesy of the British Museum ▪ Page 46, Louvre Museum, Paris ▪ Page 99, NASA photo ▪ Page 114, Smithsonian Institution, Washington, D.C.; photo number 83-2259 ▪ Page 115, By courtesy of U.S. National Library of Medicine ▪ Page 121, Aerial Photography Archives, Geography Department, Hebrew University, Jerusalem ▪ Page 137, Left, U.S. Army photo ▪ Page 137, Right, British Aerospace, Aircraft Group, Warton Division ▪ Page 138, FAO photo ▪ Page 143, WHO photo

Chapter 1

Why Read the Bible?

We are living in a world with too many problems and far too few answers. Many millions regularly go hungry. Increasing numbers are addicted to drugs. More and more families are breaking up. Incest and family violence are constantly in the news. The air we breathe and the water we drink are slowly being poisoned. Meanwhile, more and more of us are victimized by crime. Do you think problems like these will ever be solved?

IN ADDITION, we live in an age of hard choices. Many, for example, are implacably opposed to abortion, calling it murder of the unborn. Others feel just as strongly that women have authority over their own bodies and should decide such a matter for themselves. Many view homosexuality, adultery, and premarital sex as rank immorality. Others believe these practices are a matter of personal choice. Who is to say who is right and who is wrong?

2 The Bible offers guidance in matters of morality, and it describes effective solutions to the problems of crime, hunger, and pollution. The trouble is, most people no longer view the Bible as an authority in such matters. At one time, it was

---

1. (Include introduction.) What modern problems show that mankind needs guidance?
2, 3. How do many today view the Bible?

The Bible is the most widely distributed and the most translated book in all history

listened to with respect—at least in the West. Although the Bible was written down by humans, in the past the majority in Christendom accepted it as the Word of God and believed that God himself had inspired its contents.

3 Today, however, it is fashionable to be skeptical about everything: customs, ideas, morals, even the existence of God. Especially, people doubt the value of the Bible. Most seem to consider it out of date and irrelevant. Few modern intellectuals view it as the Word of God. Most people would rather agree with scholar James Barr, who wrote: "My account of the formation of the biblical tradition is an account of a *human* work. It is *man's* statement of his beliefs."[1]

4 Is this your opinion? Do you think the Bible is God's word, or man's? However you answer that question, consider this point: If the Bible is merely man's word, then logically there *is* no clear answer

---

4, 5. Why is it vital to know whether the Bible is inspired by God or not? What is the purpose of this publication?

to mankind's problems. Humans will just have to muddle through as best they can, hoping somehow to avoid poisoning themselves out of existence or blowing themselves up in a nuclear war. But if the Bible *is* the Word of God, it is the very thing we need to get us through this difficult time.

5 This publication will present evidence that the Bible really is God's Word. And the publishers hope that after you have considered the evidence, you will realize that the Bible contains the only valid answers to mankind's problems. First, though, we would like to draw to your attention some facts that, in themselves, make the Bible worthy of your consideration.

An All-Time Best-Seller

6 To begin with, it is a best-seller, the most widely circulated book in all history. According to the 1988 edition of the *Guinness Book of World Records,* an estimated 2,500,000,000 copies were printed between 1815 and 1975. That is an enormous figure. No other book in history has come even close to the Bible in circulation figures.

7 Besides that, no other book has been translated into so many languages. The Bible can now be read, in its entirety or in part, in more than 1,800 different tongues. The American Bible Society reports that it is now accessible to 98 percent of the population of our planet. Imagine the huge effort involved in producing so many translations! What other book has received such attention?

6, 7. What remarkable facts about the Bible demand our attention?

A Book With Influence

8 *The New Encyclopædia Britannica* calls the Bible "probably the most influential collection of books in human history."[2] The 19th-century German poet Heinrich Heine confessed: "I owe my enlightenment quite simply to the reading of a book . . . the Bible. It is quite rightly called Holy Scriptures. He who has lost his God can rediscover Him in this book."[3] During that same century, antislavery activist William H. Seward proclaimed: "The whole hope of human progress is suspended on the ever-growing influence of the Bible."[4]

9 Abraham Lincoln, the 16th president of the United States, called the Bible "the best gift God has ever given to man . . . But for it we could not know right from wrong."[5] British jurist Sir William Blackstone highlighted the influence of the Bible when he said: "Upon these two foundations, the law of nature and the law of revelation [the Bible], depend all human laws, that is to say, no human laws should be suffered to contradict these."[6]

Hated and Loved

10 At the same time, we have to note that no other book has been the target of so much vicious opposition and even hatred throughout history. Bibles have been burned on public bonfires, from the Middle Ages down to our 20th century. And reading or distributing the Bible has been punished with fines and imprisonment even in modern times. In past centuries, such "crimes" often led to torture and death.

8, 9. What expressions have some made that show the influence the Bible has exercised?

10. How has opposition to the Bible been expressed?

11 Parallel with this has been the devotion that the Bible has inspired. Many have persevered in reading it despite relentless persecution. Consider William Tyndale, a 16th-century Englishman who was educated at Oxford University and became a respected instructor at Cambridge University.

12 Tyndale loved the Bible. But in his days, the religious authorities insisted on keeping it in Latin, a dead language. So, in order to make it accessible to his fellow countrymen, Tyndale determined to translate the Bible into English. Since this was against the law, Tyndale had to give up his comfortable academic career and flee to the Continent. He lived the difficult life of a fugitive long enough to translate the Greek Scriptures (the "New Testament") and some of the Hebrew Scriptures (the "Old Testament") into his native tongue; but he was finally arrested, convicted of heresy, and strangled, and his body was burned.

13 Tyndale is only one of a great number of people who have sacrificed everything in order to read

---

11, 12. How did Tyndale demonstrate his love of the Bible?
13. What is one thing that makes the Bible truly unique?

As this 15th-century woodcut illustrates, many were burned alive for the "crime" of reading the Bible

the Bible or make it available to others. No other book has inspired so many ordinary men and women to rise to such heights of courage. In this respect, the Bible is truly without equal.

Claim That It Is God's Word

14 The Bible is also unique because of the claim made by many of its writers. Some 40 individuals, including kings, shepherds, fishermen, civil servants, priests, at least one general, and a physician, had a hand in writing the different parts of the Bible. But time and again, the writers made the same claim: that they were writing not their own thoughts but God's.

15 Thus, in the Bible we often read expressions such as: "The spirit of Jehovah it was that spoke by me, and his word was upon my tongue" or, "This is what the Sovereign Lord, Jehovah of armies, has said." (2 Samuel 23:2; Isaiah 22:15) In a letter sent to a fellow evangelizer, the apostle Paul wrote: "All Scripture is inspired of God and beneficial for teaching, for reproving, for setting things straight, for disciplining in righteousness, that the man of God may be fully competent, completely equipped for every good work."—2 Timothy 3:16, 17.

16 In harmony with the claim that it is God's word, not man's, the Bible answers questions that only God can answer. It explains, for example, why human governments have not been able to bring lasting peace, how humans can find the deepest satisfaction in life, and what the future holds for

---

14, 15. What claim do Bible writers frequently make?
16. What questions does the Bible discuss?

Bible writers claimed to be inspired by God

the earth and mankind upon it. Now, as a thinking person, you must have wondered about these and similar questions many times. Why not at least *consider* the possibility that the Bible is God's Word and thus uniquely able to give authoritative answers?

17 We encourage you to examine carefully the evidence presented in this book. Some of its chapters will discuss often-heard criticisms of the Bible. Is the Bible unscientific? Does it contradict itself? Does it contain real history or just myth? Did the miracles recorded in the Bible really happen? Logical evidence is presented to answer these questions. After this, powerful demonstrations of the Bible's divine inspiration are discussed: its prophecies, its deep wisdom, and the remarkable effect it has on people's lives. Finally, we will see what effect the Bible can have on *your* life.

18 First, though, we will discuss how we got the Bible. Even the history of this amazing book gives proof that it has more than merely a human origin.

17, 18. (a) What are some of the accusations leveled against the Bible that are discussed in this publication? (b) What further subjects will be covered?

Chapter 2

The Bible's Fight to Live

There are many strands of evidence proving that the Bible really is God's Word. Each strand is strong, but when all are taken together, they are unbreakable. In this chapter and the one following, we will discuss just one strand of evidence: the history of the Bible as a book. The truth is, it is nothing short of a miracle that this remarkable book has survived until today. Consider the facts for yourself.

THE Bible is more than just a book. It is a rich library of 66 books, some short and some quite long, containing law, prophecy, history, poetry, counsel, and much more. Centuries before the birth of Christ, the first 39 of these books were written—mostly in the Hebrew language—by faithful Jews, or Israelites. This part is often called the Old Testament. The last 27 books were written in Greek by Christians and are widely known as the New Testament. According to internal evidence and the most ancient traditions, these 66 books were written over a period of about 1,600 years, beginning when Egypt was a domi-

1. What are some details about the Bible?

nant power and ending when Rome was mistress of the world.

Only the Bible Survived

2 More than 3,000 years ago, when the writing of the Bible got started, Israel was just one small nation among many in the Middle East. Jehovah was their God, while the surrounding nations had a bewildering variety of gods and goddesses. During that period of time, the Israelites were not the only ones to produce religious literature. Other nations too produced written works that reflected their religion and their national values. For example, the Akkadian legend of Gilgamesh from Mesopotamia and the Ras Shamra epics, written in Ugaritic (a language spoken in what is now northern Syria), were doubtless very popular. The vast literature of that era also included works such as *The Admonitions of Ipu-wer* and *The Prophecy of Nefer-rohu* in the Egyptian language, hymns to different divinities in Sumerian, and prophetic works in Akkadian.[1]

2. (a) What was the situation of Israel when the Bible started to be written? (b) What were some other written works that were produced during the same time period?

The Hebrews were a small nation constantly threatened by stronger nations. This ancient carving pictures some Hebrews being led off captive by the Assyrians

Before the advent of printing, the Scriptures were copied by hand

[3] All these Middle Eastern works, however, met a common fate. They were forgotten, and even the languages they were written in became extinct. It was only in recent years that archaeologists and philologists learned of their existence and discovered how to read them. On the other hand, the first written books of the Hebrew Bible have survived right up to our own time and are still widely read. Sometimes scholars claim that the Hebrew books in the Bible were derived in some way from those ancient literary works. But the fact that so much of that literature was forgotten while the Hebrew Bible survived marks the Bible as significantly different.

The Guardians of the Word

[4] Make no mistake, from a human standpoint the survival of the Bible was not a foregone conclusion. The communities that produced it suffered such difficult trials and bitter oppression that its survival to our day is truly remarkable. In the years before Christ, the Jews who produced the Hebrew Scriptures (the "Old Testament") were a

---

3. What marks the Bible as different from other religious literature produced in the Middle East during the same period?

4. What grave problems of the Israelites may have seemed to put the Bible's survival in doubt?

relatively small nation. They dwelt precariously amid powerful political states that were jostling with one another for supremacy. Israel had to fight for its life against a succession of nations, such as the Philistines, the Moabites, the Ammonites, and the Edomites. During a period when the Hebrews were divided into two kingdoms, the cruel Assyrian Empire virtually wiped out the northern kingdom, while the Babylonians destroyed the southern kingdom, taking the people into an exile from which only a remnant returned 70 years later.

5 There are even reports of attempted genocide against the Israelites. Back in the days of Moses, Pharaoh ordered the murder of all their newborn baby boys. If his order had been observed, the Hebrew people would have been annihilated. (Exodus 1:15-22) Much later, when the Jews came under Persian rule, their enemies plotted to get a law passed intended to exterminate them. (Esther 3:1-15) The failure of this scheme is still celebrated in the Jewish Festival of Purim.

6 Later still, when the Jews were subject to Syria, King Antiochus IV tried very hard to Hellenize the nation, forcing it to follow Greek customs and worship Greek gods. He too failed. Instead of being wiped out or assimilated, the Jews survived while, one after the other, most of the national groups around them disappeared from the world scene. And the Hebrew Scriptures of the Bible survived with them.

5, 6. What attempts were made that endangered the very existence of the Hebrews as a distinct people?

Nero made being a Christian a capital offense

[7] The Christians, who produced the second part of the Bible (the "New Testament"), were also an oppressed group. Their leader, Jesus, was killed like a common criminal. In the early days after his death, Jewish authorities in Palestine tried to suppress them. When Christianity spread to other lands, the Jews hounded them, trying to hinder their missionary work.—Acts 5:27, 28; 7:58-60; 11:19-21; 13:45; 14:19; 18:5, 6.

[8] In the time of Nero, the initially tolerant attitude of the Roman authorities changed. Tacitus boasted of the "exquisite tortures" inflicted on Christians by that vicious emperor, and from his time on, being a Christian was a capital offense.[2] In 303 C.E., Emperor Diocletian acted directly against the Bible.* In an effort to stamp out Christianity, he ordered that all Christian Bibles should be burned.[3]

[9] These campaigns of oppression and genocide were a real threat to the Bible's survival. If the

* In this publication, instead of the traditional "A.D." and "B.C.," the more accurate "C.E." (Common Era) and "B.C.E." (before the Common Era) are used.

7, 8. How was the survival of the Bible threatened by the tribulations of the Christians?

9. What would have happened if campaigns of extermination against the Jews and the Christians had succeeded?

Jews had gone the way of the Philistines and the Moabites or if the efforts of first the Jewish and then the Roman authorities to stamp out Christianity had succeeded, who would have written and preserved the Bible? Happily, the guardians of the Bible—first the Jews and then the Christians—were not wiped out, and the Bible survived. There was, however, another serious threat if not to the survival at least to the integrity of the Bible.

Fallible Copies

10 Many of the aforementioned ancient works that were subsequently forgotten had been engraved in stone or stamped on durable clay tablets. Not so the Bible. This was originally written on papyrus or on parchment—much more perishable materials. Thus, the manuscripts produced by the original writers disappeared long, long ago. How, then, was the Bible preserved? Countless thousands of copies were laboriously written out by hand. This was the normal way to reproduce a book before the advent of printing.

11 There is, however, a danger in copying by hand. Sir Frederic Kenyon, the famous archaeologist and librarian of the British Museum, explained: "The human hand and brain have not yet been created which could copy the whole of a long work absolutely without error. . . . Mistakes were certain to creep in."[4] When a mistake crept into a

10. How was the Bible originally preserved?
11. What inevitably happens when manuscripts are copied by hand?

manuscript, it was repeated when *that* manuscript became the basis for future copies. When many copies were made over a long period of time, numerous human errors crept in.

12 In view of the many thousands of copies of the Bible that were made, how do we know that this reproduction process did not change it beyond all recognition? Well, take the case of the Hebrew Bible, the "Old Testament." In the second half of the sixth century B.C.E., when the Jews returned from their Babylonian exile, a group of Hebrew scholars known as Sopherim, "scribes," became the custodians of the Hebrew Bible text, and it was their responsibility to copy those Scriptures for use in public and private worship. They were highly motivated, professional men, and their work was of the highest quality.

13 From the seventh century to the tenth century of our Common Era, the heirs of the Sopherim were the Masoretes. Their name comes from a Hebrew word meaning "tradition," and essentially they too were scribes charged with the task of preserving the traditional Hebrew text.The Masoretes were meticulous. For example, the scribe had to use a properly authenticated copy as his master text, and he was not allowed to write anything from memory. He had to check each letter before writing it.[5] Professor Norman K. Gottwald reports: "Something of the care with which they discharged their duties is indicated in the rabbinic

---

12, 13. Who assumed responsibility for preserving the text of the Hebrew Scriptures?

The Bible's Well-Established Text

To appreciate how well established the text of the Bible is, we have only to compare it with another body of literature that has come to us from antiquity: the classical writings of Greece and Rome. In fact, most of this literature was written after the Hebrew Scriptures were completed. There were no recorded genocide attempts against the Greeks or the Romans, and their literature was not preserved in the face of persecution. Yet, notice the comments of Professor F. F. Bruce:

"For Cæsar's *Gallic War* (composed between 58 and 50 B.C.) there are several extant MSS, but only nine or ten are good, and the oldest is some 900 years later than Cæsar's day.

"Of the 142 books of the Roman history of Livy (59 B.C.-A.D. 17), only 35 survive; these are known to us from not more than twenty MSS of any consequence, only one of which, and that containing fragments of Books III-VI, is as old as the fourth century.

"Of the fourteen books of the *Histories* of Tacitus (*c.* A.D. 100) only four and a half survive; of the sixteen books of his *Annals,* ten survive in full and two in part. The text of these extant portions of his two great historical works depends entirely on two MSS, one of the ninth century and one of the eleventh. . . .

"The History of Thucydides (*c.* 460-400 B.C.) is known to us from eight MSS, the earliest belonging to *c.* A.D. 900, and a few papyrus scraps, belonging to about the beginning of the Christian era.

"The same is true of the History of Herodotus (*c.* 488-428 B.C.). Yet no classical scholar would listen to an argument that the authenticity of Herodotus or Thucydides is in doubt because the earliest MSS of their works which are of any use to us are over 1,300 years later than the originals."—*The Books and the Parchments,* page 180.

Compare this with the fact that there are thousands of manuscripts of various parts of the Bible. And manuscripts of the Christian Greek Scriptures go back to within a hundred years of the time of the writing of the original books.

requirement that all new manuscripts were to be proofread and defective copies discarded at once."[6]

[14] How accurate was the transmission of the text by the Sopherim and the Masoretes? Until 1947 it was difficult to answer that question, since the earliest available complete Hebrew manuscripts were from the tenth century of our Common Era. In 1947, however, some very ancient manuscript fragments were found in caves in the vicinity of the Dead Sea, including parts of books of the Hebrew Bible. A number of fragments dated to before the time of Christ. Scholars compared these with existing Hebrew manuscripts to confirm the accuracy of the transmission of the text. What was the result of this comparison?

[15] One of the oldest works discovered was the complete book of Isaiah, and the closeness of its text to that of the Masoretic Bible we have today is amazing. Professor Millar Burrows writes: "Many of the differences between the [recently discovered] St. Mark's Isaiah scroll and the Masoretic text can be explained as mistakes in copying. Apart from these, there is a remarkable agreement, on the whole, with the text found in the medieval manuscripts. Such agreement in a manuscript so much older gives reassuring testimony to the general accuracy of the traditional text."[7] Bur-

14. What discovery made it possible to confirm the transmission of the Bible text by the Sopherim and the Masoretes?
15. (a) What was the result of comparing the Dead Sea scroll manuscript of Isaiah with the Masoretic text? (b) What should we conclude from the fact that some manuscripts found at the Dead Sea show a certain amount of textual variance? (See footnote.)

A study of the Dead Sea scroll of Isaiah proved that this book had remained practically unchanged over a period of 1,000 years

rows adds: "It is a matter for wonder that through something like a thousand years the text underwent so little alteration."*

16 In the case of the part of the Bible written in Greek by Christians, the so-called New Testament, the copyists were more like gifted amateurs than like the highly trained professional Sopherim. But working as they did under the threat of punishment by the authorities, they took their work

---

* Not all the manuscripts found at the Dead Sea agreed so exactly with the surviving Bible text. Some showed quite a lot of textual variance. However, these variations do not mean that the essential meaning of the text has been distorted. According to Patrick W. Skehan of the Catholic University of America, most represent a "reworking [of the Bible text] on the basis of its own integral logic, so that the form becomes expanded but the substance remains the same . . . The underlying attitude is one of explicit reverence for a text regarded as sacred, an attitude of explaining (as we would put it) the Bible by the Bible in the very transmission of the text itself."[8]

Another commentator adds: "In spite of all uncertainties, the great fact remains that the text as we now have it does, in the main, represent fairly the actual words of the authors who lived, some of them, nearly three thousand years ago, and we need have no serious doubt on the score of textual corruption as to the validity of the message which the Old Testament has to give us."[9]

16, 17. (a) Why can we be sure that the text of the Christian Greek Scriptures is sound? (b) What did Sir Frederic Kenyon testify about the text of the Greek Scriptures?

seriously. And two things assure us that we today have a text essentially the same as that penned by the original writers. First, we have manuscripts dated much closer to the time of writing than is the case with the Hebrew part of the Bible. Indeed, one fragment of the Gospel of John is from the first half of the second century, less than 50 years from the date when John probably wrote his Gospel. Second, the sheer number of manuscripts that have survived provides a formidable demonstration of the soundness of the text.

17 On this point, Sir Frederic Kenyon testified: "It cannot be too strongly asserted that in substance the text of the Bible is certain. Especially is this the case with the New Testament. The number of manuscripts of the New Testament, of early translations from it, and of quotations from it in the oldest writers of the Church, is so large that it is practically certain that the true reading of every doubtful passage is preserved in some one or other of these ancient authorities. This can be said of no other ancient book in the world."[10]

The People and Their Languages

18 The original languages in which the Bible was written were also, in the long run, an obstacle to its survival. The first 39 books were mostly written in Hebrew, the tongue of the Israelites. But Hebrew has never been widely known. If the Bible had stayed in that language, it would never have had any influence beyond the Jewish nation and the

18, 19. How was it that the Bible was not limited to the languages in which it was originally written?

Emperor Diocletian failed in his efforts to destroy the Bible

few foreigners who could read it. However, in the third century B.C.E., for the benefit of Hebrews living in Alexandria, Egypt, translation of the Hebrew part of the Bible into Greek began. Greek was then an international language. Thus, the Hebrew Bible became easily accessible to non-Jews.

19 When the time came for the second part of the Bible to be written, Greek was still very widely spoken, so the final 27 books of the Bible were written in that tongue. But not everybody could understand Greek. Hence, translations of both the Hebrew and the Greek parts of the Bible soon began to appear in the everyday languages of those early centuries, such as Syriac, Coptic, Armenian, Georgian, Gothic, and Ethiopic. The official language of the Roman Empire was Latin, and Latin translations were made in such numbers that an "authorized version" had to be commissioned. This was completed about 405 C.E. and came to be known as the *Vulgate* (meaning "popular" or "common").

20 Thus, it was in spite of many obstacles that the Bible survived down to the early centuries of our Common Era. Those who produced it were

20, 21. What were the obstacles to the Bible's survival, and why were these overcome?

despised and persecuted minorities living a difficult existence in a hostile world. It could easily have been badly distorted in the process of copying, but it was not. Moreover, it escaped the danger of being available only to people who spoke certain languages.

21 Why was it so difficult for the Bible to survive? The Bible itself says: "The whole world is lying in the power of the wicked one." (1 John 5:19) In view of this, we would expect the world to be hostile to published truth, and this has proved to be the case. Why, then, *did* the Bible survive when so many other pieces of literature that did not face the same difficulties were forgotten? The Bible answers this too. It says: "The saying of Jehovah endures forever." (1 Peter 1:25) If the Bible really is the Word of God, no human power can destroy it. And right up into this 20th century, this has been true.

22 However, in the fourth century of our Common Era, something happened that eventually resulted in new attacks on the Bible and profoundly affected the course of European history. Just ten years after Diocletian tried to destroy all copies of the Bible, imperial policy changed and "Christianity" was legalized. Twelve years later, in 325 C.E., a Roman emperor presided over the "Christian" Council of Nicaea. Why would such a seemingly favorable development prove to be hazardous for the Bible? We will see the answer in the following chapter.

---

22. What change took place early in the fourth century of our Common Era?

Chapter 3

The Bible's False Friend

In this chapter, we discuss the major reason why many from non-Christian lands refuse to accept the Bible as the Word of God. Historically, Christendom has claimed to believe in the Bible and to be its guardian. But the religious organizations of Christendom have been associated with some of the most appalling horrors of history, from the Crusades and pogroms of the Middle Ages to the Holocaust of our own time. Is the conduct of Christendom a good reason to reject the Bible? The truth is, Christendom has proved to be a false friend of the Bible. Indeed, when Christendom emerged in the fourth century C.E., the Bible's fight to survive was by no means over.

BY THE end of the first century, the writing of all the books of the Bible was completed. From then on, Christians were in the forefront of copying and distributing the complete Bible. At the same time, they were busy translating it into the most common languages of the day. While the Christian congregation was busy with this

1, 2. (Include introduction.) (a) Why do many refuse to accept the Bible as the Word of God? (b) What good work was accomplished during the first and second centuries, yet what dangerous development was under way?

The history of Christendom really began when Constantine legalized the "Christianity" of his day

admirable work, however, something was beginning to take shape that would prove very dangerous to the survival of the Bible.

[2] This development was foretold by the Bible itself. Jesus once told a parable of a man who sowed his field with good quality seeds of wheat. But "while men were sleeping," an enemy sowed seeds that would produce weeds. Both types of seeds sprouted, and for a while the weeds hid the wheat from view. By this parable, Jesus showed that the fruitage of his work would be true Christians but that after his death, false Christians would infiltrate the congregation. Eventually, it would be difficult to distinguish the genuine from the false. —Matthew 13:24-30, 36-43.

[3] The apostle Peter frankly warned of the effect of these weedlike "Christians" on the way people would view Christianity and the Bible. He warned: "There will also be false teachers among you. These very ones will quietly bring in destructive sects and will disown even the owner that bought them, bringing speedy destruction upon themselves. Furthermore, many will follow their acts of loose conduct, and *on account of these the way of the truth will be spoken of abusively.*"—2 Peter 2:1, 2.

---

3. According to the apostle Peter, what would be the effect of weedlike "Christians" on belief in the Bible?

[4] Even during the first century, the prophecies of Jesus and Peter were being fulfilled. Ambitious men infiltrated the Christian congregation and sowed dissension. (2 Timothy 2:16-18; 2 Peter 2:21, 22; 3 John 9, 10) During the following two centuries, the purity of Bible truth was corrupted by Greek philosophy, and many mistakenly came to accept pagan doctrines as Bible truth.

[5] In the fourth century, the Roman emperor Constantine adopted "Christianity" as the official religion of the Roman Empire. But the "Christianity" he knew was very different from the religion preached by Jesus. By now, the "weeds" were flourishing, just as Jesus had foretold. Nevertheless, we can be sure that during all that time, there were some who represented true Christianity and labored to follow the Bible as the inspired Word of God.—Matthew 28:19, 20.

Bible Translation Opposed

[6] It was in Constantine's time that Christendom as we know it today began to take shape. From then on, the degenerate form of Christianity that had taken root was no longer just a religious organization. It was a part of the state, and its leaders played an important role in politics. Eventually, the apostate church used its political power in a way that was completely opposed to Bible

---

4. How were the prophecies of Jesus and Peter fulfilled even during the first century?

5. What policy change did Constantine inaugurate early in the fourth century?

6. When did Christendom begin to take shape, and what was one way in which Christendom's religion differed from Bible Christianity?

Christianity, introducing another dangerous threat to the Bible. How?

7 When Latin died out as an everyday tongue, new translations of the Bible were needed. But the Catholic Church no longer favored this. In 1079 Vratislaus, who later became king of Bohemia, asked the permission of Pope Gregory VII to translate the Bible into the language of his subjects. The pope's answer was no. He stated: "It is clear to those who reflect often upon it, that not without reason has it pleased Almighty God that holy scripture should be a secret in certain places, lest, if it were plainly apparent to all men, perchance it would be little esteemed and be subject to disrespect; or it might be falsely understood by those of mediocre learning, and lead to error."[1]

8 The pope wanted the Bible to be kept in the now-dead tongue of Latin. Its contents were to be kept "secret," not translated into the languages of the common people.* Jerome's Latin *Vulgate,* produced in the 5th century to make the Bible accessible to all, now became a means of keeping it hidden.

9 As the Middle Ages progressed, the Church's stand against vernacular Bibles hardened. In 1199 Pope Innocent III wrote such a strong letter to the

---

* A few translations into vernacular languages were made. But they were often laboriously produced in very ornate manuscripts and were definitely not for popular use.[2]

7, 8. When did the pope express opposition to the translating of the Bible, and why did he do this?

9, 10. (a) How did Roman Catholic opposition to Bible translation develop? (b) What was the purpose of the Church's opposition to the Bible?

Popes Gregory VII and Innocent III were prominent in the Catholic Church's struggle to prevent the Bible from being translated into the everyday language of the people

archbishop of Metz, Germany, that the archbishop burned all the German-language Bibles he could find.[3] In 1229 the synod of Toulouse, France, decreed that "lay people" could not possess any Bible books in the common tongue.[4] In 1233 a provincial synod of Tarragona, Spain, commanded that all books of "the Old or New Testament" be handed over to be burned.[5] In 1407 the synod of clergy summoned in Oxford, England, by Archbishop Thomas Arundel expressly forbade the translating of the Bible into English or any other modern tongue.[6] In 1431, also in England, Bishop Stafford of Wells forbade the translating of the Bible into English and the owning of such translations.[7]

10 These religious authorities were not trying to destroy the Bible. They were trying to fossilize it, keep it in a language that only a few could read. In this way, they hoped to prevent what they called heresy but what really amounted to challenges to their authority. If they had succeeded, the Bible could have become just an object of intellectual curiosity, with little or no influence in the lives of ordinary people.

The Bible's Champions

11 Happily, though, many sincere people refused to follow these edicts. But such refusals were dangerous. Individuals suffered terribly for the "crime" of owning a Bible. Consider, as an example, the case of a Spaniard named Julián Hernández. According to Foxe's *History of Christian Martyrdom,* Julián (or, Juliano) "undertook to convey from Germany into his own country a great number of Bibles, concealed in casks, and packed up like Rhenish wine." He was betrayed and seized by the Roman Catholic Inquisition. Those for whom the Bibles were destined "were all indiscriminately tortured, and then most of them were sentenced to various punishments. Juliano was burnt, twenty were roasted upon spits, several imprisoned for life, some were publicly whipped, many sent to the galleys."[8]

12 What a horrible abuse of power! Clearly, these religious authorities were by no means representative of Bible Christianity! The Bible itself revealed to whom they belonged when it said: "The children of God and the children of the Devil are evident by this fact: Everyone who does not carry on righteousness does not originate with God, neither does he who does not love his brother. For this is the message which you have heard from the beginning, that we should have love for one another; not like Cain, who originated with the wicked one and slaughtered his brother."—1 John 3:10-12.

---

11. What resulted when Julián Hernández smuggled Spanish-language Bibles into Spain?

12. How do we know that the religious authorities of the Middle Ages did not represent Bible Christianity?

13 How remarkable, though, that men and women were willing to risk such shocking treatment just to possess a Bible! And such examples have been multiplied many times over right down to our day. The deep devotion that the Bible has inspired in individuals, the willingness to suffer patiently and to submit uncomplainingly to terrible deaths without striking back at their tormentors, is a strong evidence that the Bible *is* the Word of God. —1 Peter 2:21.

14 Eventually, after the Protestant rebellion against Roman Catholic power in the 16th century, the Roman Catholic Church itself was forced to produce translations of the Bible in the everyday languages of Europe. But even then, the Bible was associated more with Protestantism than with Catholicism. As Roman Catholic priest Edward J. Ciuba wrote: "One would honestly have to admit that one of the more tragic consequences of the Protestant Reformation was a neglect of the Bible among the Catholic faithful. While it was never completely forgotten, the Bible was a closed book for most Catholics."[9]

Higher Criticism

15 But the Protestant churches are not free from blame as far as opposing the Bible is concerned. As the years passed, certain Protestant scholars mounted another sort of attack on the

---

13, 14. (a) What remarkable fact about the Bible during the Middle Ages shows its divine origin? (b) How did the situation change as far as the Bible was concerned in Europe?

15, 16. Why is Protestantism not free from blame as far as opposition to the Bible is concerned?

book: an intellectual attack. During the 18th and 19th centuries, they developed a method of studying the Bible known as higher criticism. Higher critics taught that much of the Bible was composed of legend and myth. Some even said that Jesus never existed. Instead of being designated the Word of God, the Bible was said by these Protestant scholars to be the word of man, and a very jumbled word at that.

16 While the more extreme of these ideas are no longer believed, higher criticism is still taught in seminaries, and it is not unusual to hear Protestant clergymen publicly disavow large sections of the Bible. Thus, one Anglican clergyman was quoted in an Australian newspaper as saying that much that is in the Bible "is just wrong. Some of the history is wrong. Some of the details are obviously garbled." This thinking is a product of higher criticism.

"Spoken of Abusively"

17 Perhaps, though, it is the conduct of Christendom that has posed the greatest obstacle to people's accepting the Bible as God's Word. Christendom claims to follow the Bible. Yet, her conduct has brought great reproach on the Bible and on the very name Christian. As the apostle Peter foretold, the way of the truth has been "spoken of abusively."—2 Peter 2:2.

18 For example, while the church was banning Bible translation, the pope was sponsoring massive

---

17, 18. How has the conduct of Christendom brought reproach on the Bible?

The shocking conduct of Christendom has led many to doubt that the Bible is really the Word of God

military efforts against the Muslims in the Middle East. These came to be called "holy" Crusades, but there was nothing holy about them. The first —termed the "People's Crusade"—set the tone for what was to come. Before leaving Europe, an unruly army, inflamed by preachers, turned on the Jews in Germany, slaughtering them in one town after another. Why? Historian Hans Eberhard Mayer says: "The argument that the Jews, as the enemies of Christ, deserved to be punished was merely a feeble attempt to conceal the real motive: greed."[10]

19 The Protestant rebellion in the 16th century dislodged Roman Catholicism from power in many European lands. One result was the Thirty Years' War (1618-48)—"one of the most terrible wars in

---

19-21. How did the Thirty Years' War, as well as Europe's missionary endeavors and colonial expansion, serve to bring reproach on the Bible?

European history," according to *The Universal History of the World.* The basic cause of the war? "The hatred of Catholic for Protestant, of Protestant for Catholic."[11]

20 By this time, Christendom had begun to expand beyond Europe, carrying "Christian" civilization into other parts of the earth. This military expansion was marked by cruelty and greed. In the Americas, the Spanish conquistadores quickly destroyed the indigenous American civilizations. Noted one history book: "In general, the Spanish governors destroyed the native civilization, without introducing the European. The thirst for gold was the principal motive that drew them to the New World."[12]

21 Protestant missionaries also went out from Europe to other continents. One of the results of their work was the promotion of colonial expansion. A widespread view today of the Protestant missionary effort is: "In many instances the missionary enterprise has been used as a justification and a cover for the domination of people. The interrelation between mission, technology, and imperialism is well known."[13]

The mainstream Protestant churches have shared in a major intellectual assault on the Bible

22 The close association between Christendom's religions and the state has continued down to our

22. How has Christendom brought reproach on the name of Christianity during the 20th century?

During the first world war, these Russian soldiers bow to a religious icon before going out to kill fellow "Christians"

day. The last two world wars were fought primarily between "Christian" nations. Clergymen on both sides encouraged their young men to fight and try to kill the enemy—who often belonged to the same religion. As was noted in the book *If the Churches Want World Peace:* "Certainly it is no credit to [the churches] that the war system of today grew up and has worked its greatest havoc among states devoted to the cause of Christianity."[14]

The Word of God Survives

23 We recount this long, sad history of Christendom to highlight two points. First, such events are a fulfillment of Bible prophecy. It was foretold

---

23. How does the history of Christendom indicate that the Bible is God's Word?

that many claiming to be Christian would bring reproach on the Bible and the name of Christianity, and the fact that this has happened vindicates the Bible as being true. Nevertheless, we should not lose sight of the fact that *the conduct of Christendom does not represent Bible-based Christianity.*

24 The way genuine Christians can be recognized was explained by Jesus himself: "By this all will know that you are my disciples, if you have love among yourselves." (John 13:35) Further, Jesus said: "They are no part of the world, just as I am no part of the world." (John 17:16) On both counts, Christendom betrays itself as clearly not representing Bible Christianity. It claims to be the Bible's friend, but it has been a false friend.

25 The second point is this: In view of the fact that Christendom as a whole has acted so much against the interests of the Bible, it is remarkable, indeed, that the book has survived until today and still exercises a good influence on many people's lives. The Bible has survived bitter opposition to translating it, onslaughts from modernistic scholars, and the unchristian conduct of its false friend, Christendom. Why? Because the Bible is unlike any other written work. The Bible *cannot* die. It is the Word of God, and the Bible itself tells us: "The grass withers, the flowers fade, but the word of our God endures for evermore."—Isaiah 40:8, *The New English Bible.*

---

24. What identifies true Christians and thus clearly condemns Christendom as unchristian?

25. Why did the Bible survive all its tribulations down to our time?

Chapter 4

How Believable Is the "Old Testament"?

In the next few chapters, we will discuss some of the charges leveled against the Bible by modern critics. Some charge that the Bible contradicts itself and is "unscientific," and these accusations will be taken up later. But first, consider the often-made charge that the Bible is no more than a collection of myths and legends. Do the Bible's opponents have solid grounds for such a criticism? To begin with, let us look at the Hebrew Scriptures, the so-called Old Testament.

AN ANCIENT city is under siege. Its attackers have swarmed across the Jordan River and are now encamped before the city's high walls. But what strange battle tactics! Each day for six days, the invading army has marched around the city, silent except for an accompanying group of priests blowing on horns. Now, on the seventh day, the army silently marches around the city seven times. Suddenly, the priests blow their horns with all their might. The army breaks its silence with a mighty battle cry, and the towering city walls collapse in a cloud of dust, leaving the city defenseless.—Joshua 6:1-21.

1, 2. What was the siege of Jericho like, and what questions are raised in connection with it?

[2] This is how the book of Joshua, the sixth book of the Hebrew Scriptures, describes the fall of Jericho that occurred almost 3,500 years ago. But did it really happen? Many higher critics would confidently answer no.* They claim that the book of Joshua, along with the previous five books of the Bible, is made up of legends written up many centuries after the alleged events took place. Many archaeologists would also answer no. According to them, when the Israelites came into the land of Canaan, Jericho may not even have existed.

[3] These are serious charges. As you read through the Bible, you will notice that its teachings are solidly linked to history. God deals with real men, women, families, and nations, and his commands are given to a historical people. Modern scholars who cast doubt on the historicity of the Bible cast doubt also on the importance and reliability of its message. If the Bible really is God's Word, then its history must be trustworthy and not contain mere legends and myths. Do these critics have grounds for challenging its historical truthfulness?

Higher Criticism—How Reliable?

[4] Higher criticism of the Bible got started in

* "Higher criticism" (or "the historical-critical method") is a term used to describe the study of the Bible with a view to finding out details such as the authorship, source material, and time of composition of each book.

3. Why is it important to discuss whether the Bible contains true history or not?

4-6. What are some of Wellhausen's theories of higher criticism?

earnest during the 18th and 19th centuries. In the latter half of the 19th century, the German Bible critic Julius Wellhausen popularized the theory that the first six books of the Bible, including Joshua, were written in the fifth century B.C.E. —about a thousand years after the events described. He did say, though, that they contained material that had been written down earlier.[1] This theory was printed in the 11th edition of the *Encyclopædia Britannica,* published in 1911, which explained: "Genesis is a post-exilic work composed of a post-exilic priestly source (P) and non-priestly earlier sources which differ markedly from P in language, style and religious standpoint."

5 Wellhausen and his followers viewed all the history recorded in the earlier part of the Hebrew Scriptures as "not literal history, but popular traditions of the past."[2] The earlier accounts were considered to be merely a reflection of the later history of Israel. For example, it was stated that the enmity between Jacob and Esau did not really happen, but it reflected the enmity between the nations of Israel and Edom in later times.

6 In harmony with this, these critics felt that Moses never received any commandment to make the ark of the covenant and that the tabernacle, center of Israelite worship in the wilderness, never existed. They also believed that the authority of the Aaronic priesthood was fully established only a few years before the destruction of Jerusalem by the Babylonians, which the critics believed happened at the beginning of the sixth century B.C.E.[3]

[7] What "proof" did they have for these ideas? Higher critics claim to be able to divide the text of the early books of the Bible into a number of different documents. A basic principle they use is to assume that, generally speaking, any Bible verse using the Hebrew word for God (*'Elo·him'*) on its own was written by one writer, while any verse referring to God by his name, Jehovah, must have been written by another—as if one writer could not use both terms.[4]

[8] Similarly, anytime an event is recorded more than once in a book, it is taken as proof of more than one writer at work, even though ancient Semitic literature has other similar examples of repetition. Additionally, it is assumed that any change of style means a change of writer. Yet, even modern-language writers often write in different styles at different stages in their careers, or when they are dealing with different subject matter.*

[9] Is there any real proof for these theories? Not at all. One commentator noted: "Criticism, even at its best, is speculative and tentative, something always liable to be modified or proved wrong and having to be replaced by something else. It is an intellectual exercise, subject to all the doubts and guesses which are inseparable from such

---

* For example, the English poet John Milton wrote his lofty epic poem "Paradise Lost" in quite a different style from his poem "L'Allegro." And his political tracts were written in still another style.

7, 8. What "proofs" did Wellhausen have for his theories, and were they sound?

9-11. What are some outstanding weaknesses of modern higher criticism?

Milton wrote in different styles, not just one. Do higher critics believe his work to be the product of a number of different writers?

exercises."[5] Biblical higher criticism, especially, is "speculative and tentative" in the extreme.

10 Gleason L. Archer, Jr., shows another flaw in the reasoning of higher criticism. The problem, he says, is that "the Wellhausen school started with the pure assumption (which they have hardly bothered to demonstrate) that Israel's religion was of merely human origin like any other, and that it was to be explained as a mere product of evolution."[6] In other words, Wellhausen and his followers started with the assumption that the Bible was merely the word of man, and then they reasoned from there.

11 Back in 1909, *The Jewish Encyclopedia* noted two more weaknesses in the Wellhausian theory: "The arguments by which Wellhausen has almost entirely captured the whole body of contemporary Biblical critics are based on two assumptions: first, that ritual becomes more elaborate in the development of religion; secondly, that older sources necessarily deal with the earlier stages of ritual development. The former

assumption is against the evidence of primitive cultures, and the latter finds no support in the evidence of ritual codes like those of India."

[12] Is there any way of testing higher criticism to see whether its theories are correct or not? *The Jewish Encyclopedia* went on to say: "Wellhausen's views are based almost exclusively on literal analysis, and will need to be supplemented by an examination from the point of view of institutional archeology." As the years went by, did archaeology tend to confirm Wellhausen's theories? *The New Encyclopædia Britannica* answers: "Archaeological criticism has tended to substantiate the reliability of the typical historical details of even the oldest periods [of Bible history] and to discount the theory that the Pentateuchal accounts [the historical records in the earliest books of the Bible] are merely the reflection of a much later period."

[13] In view of its weakness, why is higher criticism so popular among intellectuals today? Because it tells them things that they want to hear. One 19th-century scholar explained: "Personally, I welcomed this book of Wellhausen's more than almost any other; for the pressing problem of the history of the Old Testament appeared to me to be at last solved in a manner *consonant to the principle of human evolution* which I am compelled to apply to the history of all religion."[7] Evidently, higher criticism agreed with his prejudices as an

---

12. How does modern higher criticism stand up in the light of archaeology?

13, 14. In spite of its shaky foundations, why is Wellhausen's higher criticism still widely accepted?

evolutionist. And, indeed, the two theories serve a similar end. Just as evolution would remove the need to believe in a Creator, so Wellhausen's higher criticism would mean that one does not have to believe that the Bible was inspired by God.

14 In this rationalistic 20th century, the assumption that the Bible is not God's word but man's looks plausible to intellectuals.* It is much easier for them to believe that prophecies were written after their fulfillment than to accept them as genuine. They prefer to explain away the Bible accounts of miracles as myths, legends, or folk tales, rather than consider the possibility that they really happened. But such a viewpoint is prejudiced and gives no solid reason to reject the Bible as true. Higher criticism is seriously flawed, and its assault on the Bible has failed to demonstrate that the Bible is not the Word of God.

Does Archaeology Support the Bible?

15 Archaeology is a much more solidly based field of study than higher criticism. Archaeologists, by digging among the remains of past civilizations, have in many ways increased our understanding of the way things were in ancient times. Hence, it is not surprising that the archaeological record repeatedly harmonizes with what we read in

---

* Most intellectuals today tend to be *rationalistic*. According to the dictionary, rationalism means "reliance on reason as the basis for establishment of religious truth." Rationalists try to explain everything in human terms rather than take into account the possibility of divine action.

15, 16. The existence of what ancient ruler mentioned in the Bible was confirmed by archaeology?

the Bible. Sometimes, archaeology has even vindicated the Bible against its critics.

16 For example, according to the book of Daniel, the last ruler in Babylon before it fell to the Persians was named Belshazzar. (Daniel 5:1-30) Since there appeared to be no mention of Belshazzar outside the Bible, the charge was made that the Bible was wrong and that this man never existed. But during the 19th century, several small cylinders inscribed in cuneiform were discovered in some ruins in southern Iraq. They were found to include a prayer for the health of the eldest son of Nabonidus, king of Babylon. The name of this son? Belshazzar.

17 So there was a Belshazzar! Was he a king, though, when Babylon fell? Most documents sub-

---

17. How can we explain the fact that the Bible calls Belshazzar a king, while most inscriptions called him a prince?

The Value of Archaeology

"Archaeology provides a sampling of ancient tools and vessels, walls and buildings, weapons and adornments. Most of these can be chronologically arranged and securely identified with appropriate terms and contexts contained in the Bible. In this sense the Bible accurately preserves in written form its ancient cultural milieu. The details of biblical stories are not the fanciful products of an author's imagination but rather are authentic reflections of the world in which the recorded events, from the mundane to the miraculous, took place."—*The Archaeological Encyclopedia of the Holy Land.*

The "Verse Account of Nabonidus" reports that Nabonidus entrusted the kingship to his firstborn

sequently found referred to him as the son of the king, the crown prince. But a cuneiform document described as the "Verse Account of Nabonidus" shed more light on Belshazzar's true position. It reported: "He [Nabonidus] entrusted the 'Camp' to his oldest (son), the firstborn, the troops everywhere in the country he ordered under his (command). He let (everything) go, he entrusted the kingship to him."[8] So Belshazzar was entrusted with the kingship. Surely, to all intents and purposes that made him a king!* This relationship between Belshazzar and his father, Nabonidus, explains why Belshazzar, during that final banquet in Babylon, offered to make Daniel the *third* ruler in the kingdom. (Daniel 5:16) Since Nabonidus was the first ruler, Belshazzar himself was only the second ruler of Babylon.

---

* Interestingly, a statue of an ancient ruler found in northern Syria in the 1970's showed that it was not unknown for a ruler to be called king when, strictly speaking, he had a lesser title. The statue was of a ruler of Gozan and was inscribed in Assyrian and Aramaic. The Assyrian inscription called the man governor of Gozan, but the parallel Aramaic inscription called him king.[9] So it would not be unprecedented for Belshazzar to be called crown prince in the official Babylonian inscriptions while in the Aramaic writing of Daniel he is called king.

The Moabite Stone gives King Mesha's version of the conflict between Moab and Israel

Other Supporting Evidence

18 Indeed, many archaeological discoveries have demonstrated the historical accuracy of the Bible. For example, the Bible reports that after King Solomon had taken over the kingship from his father, David, Israel enjoyed great prosperity. We read: "Judah and Israel were many, like the grains of sand that are by the sea for multitude, eating and drinking and rejoicing." (1 Kings 4:20) In support of this statement, we read: "Archaeological evidence reveals that there was a population explosion in Judah during and after the tenth century B.C. when the peace and prosperity David brought made it possible to build many new towns."[10]

19 Later on, Israel and Judah be-

Official Babylonian records support the Bible account of the fall of Jerusalem

18. What information does archaeology supply to confirm the peace and prosperity resulting from David's reign?
19. What additional information does archaeology give concerning the warfare between Israel and Moab?

came two nations, and Israel conquered the neighboring land of Moab. At one time Moab, under King Mesha, revolted, and Israel formed an alliance with Judah and the neighboring kingdom of Edom to war against Moab. (2 Kings 3:4-27) Remarkably, in 1868 in Jordan, a stela (a carved stone slab) was discovered that was inscribed in the Moabite language with Mesha's own account of this conflict.

20 Then, in the year 740 B.C.E., God allowed the rebellious northern kingdom of Israel to be destroyed by the Assyrians. (2 Kings 17:6-18) Speaking of the Bible account of this event, archaeologist Kathleen Kenyon comments: "One might have a suspicion that some of this is hyperbole." But is it? She adds: "The archaeological evidence of the fall of the kingdom of Israel is almost more vivid than that of the Biblical record. . . . The complete obliteration of the Israelite towns of Samaria and Hazor and the accompanying destruction of

---

20. What does archaeology tell us about the destruction of Israel by the Assyrians?

Megiddo is the factual archaeological evidence that the [Bible] writer was not exaggerating."[11]

21 Later still, the Bible tells us that Jerusalem under King Jehoiachin was besieged by the Babylonians and was defeated. This event is recorded on the Babylonian Chronicle, a cuneiform tablet discovered by archaeologists. On this, we read: "The king of Akkad [Babylon] . . . laid siege to the city of Judah (*iahudu*) and the king took the city on the second day of the month of Addaru."[12] Jehoiachin was taken to Babylon and imprisoned. But later, according to the Bible, he was released from prison and given an allowance of food. (2 Kings 24:8-15; 25:27-30) This is supported by administrative documents found in Babylon, which list the rations given to "Yaukîn, king of Judah."[13]

22 Regarding the relationship between archaeology and the Bible's historical accounts, Professor David Noel Freedman commented: "In general, however, archaeology has tended to support the historical validity of the biblical narrative. The broad chronological outline from the patriarchs to N[ew] T[estament] times correlates with archaeological data. . . . Future discoveries are likely to sustain the present moderate position that the biblical tradition is historically rooted, and faithfully transmitted, though it is not history in the critical or scientific sense."

23 Then, regarding the efforts of higher critics

---

21. What details about the subjugation of Judah by the Babylonians are supplied by archaeology?

22, 23. In general, what is the relationship between archaeology and the Bible's historical accounts?

to discredit the Bible, he says: "Attempted reconstructions of biblical history by modern scholars—e.g., Wellhausen's view that the patriarchal age was a reflex of the divided monarchy; or the rejection of the historicity of Moses and the exodus and consequent restructuring of Israelite history by Noth and his followers—have not survived the archaeological data as well as the biblical narrative."[14]

The Fall of Jericho

24 Does this mean that archaeology agrees with the Bible in every case? No, there are a number of disagreements. One is the dramatic conquest of Jericho described in the beginning of this chapter. According to the Bible, Jericho was the first city conquered by Joshua as he led the Israelites into the land of Canaan. Bible chronology indicates that the city fell in the first half of the 15th century B.C.E. After the conquest, Jericho was completely burned with fire and was then left uninhabited for hundreds of years.—Joshua 6:1-26; 1 Kings 16:34.

25 Before the second world war, the site believed to be Jericho was excavated by Professor John Garstang. He discovered that the city was very ancient and had been destroyed and rebuilt many times. Garstang found that during one of these destructions, the walls fell as if by earthquake, and

---

24. What information does the Bible give us about the fall of Jericho?
25, 26. What two different conclusions have archaeologists reached as a result of excavating Jericho?

the city was completely burned with fire. Garstang believed that this took place in about 1400 B.C.E., not too distant from the Biblically indicated date for the destruction of Jericho by Joshua.[15]

26 After the war, another archaeologist, Kathleen Kenyon, did further excavations at Jericho. She came to the conclusion that the collapsed walls Garstang had identified dated from hundreds of years earlier than he thought. She did identify a major destruction of Jericho in the 16th century B.C.E. but said that there was no city on the site of Jericho during the 15th century—when the Bible says Joshua was invading the land. She goes on to report *possible* indications of another destruction that might have taken place on the site in 1325 B.C.E. and suggests: "If the destruction of Jericho is to be associated with an invasion under

What Archaeology Can and Cannot Do

"Archaeology neither proves nor disproves the Bible in conclusive terms, but it has other functions, of considerable importance. It recovers in some degree the material world presupposed by the Bible. To know, say, the material of which a house was built, or what a 'high place' looked like, much enhances our understanding of the text. Secondly, it fills out the historical record. The Moabite Stone, for example, gives the other side of the story treated in 2 Kings 3:4ff. . . . Thirdly, it reveals the life and thought of the neighbours of ancient Israel—which is of interest in itself, and which illuminates the world of ideas within which the thought of ancient Israel developed."
—*Ebla—A Revelation in Archaeology.*

Joshua, this [latter] is the date that archaeology suggests."[16]

27 Does this mean that the Bible is wrong? Not at all. We have to remember that while archaeology gives us a window to the past, it is not always a clear window. Sometimes it is decidedly murky. As one commentator noted: "Archaeological evidence is, unfortunately, fragmentary, and therefore limited."[17] Especially is this true of the earlier periods of Israelite history, when archaeological evidence is not clear. Indeed, the evidence is even less clear at Jericho, since the site has been badly eroded.

The Limitations of Archaeology

28 Archaeologists themselves admit the limitations of their science. Yohanan Aharoni, for example, explains: "When it comes to historical or historio-geographical interpretation, the archaeologist steps out of the realm of the exact sciences, and he must rely upon value judgements and hypotheses to arrive at a comprehensive historical picture."[18] Regarding the dates assigned to various discoveries, he adds: "We must always remember, therefore, that not all dates are absolute and are in varying degrees suspect," although he feels that today's archaeologists can be more confident of their dating than was the case in the past.[19]

29 *The World of the Old Testament* asks the question: "How objective or truly scientific is the

---

27. Why should discrepancies between archaeology and the Bible not unduly disturb us?

28, 29. What are some limitations of archaeology that scholars have admitted?

archaeological method?" It answers: "Archaeologists are more objective when unearthing the facts than when interpreting them. But their human preoccupations will affect the methods they use in making the 'dig,' too. They cannot help destroying their evidence as they dig down through the layers of earth, so they can never test their 'experiment' by repeating it. This makes archaeology unique among the sciences. Moreover, it makes archaeological reporting a most demanding and pitfall-ridden task."[20]

30 So archaeology can be very helpful, but like any human endeavor, it is fallible. While we consider archaeological theories with interest, we should never view them as incontrovertible truth. If archaeologists interpret their findings in a way that contradicts the Bible, it should not automatically be assumed that the Bible is wrong and the archaeologists are right. Their interpretations have been known to change.

31 It is interesting to note that in 1981 Professor John J. Bimson looked again at the destruction of Jericho. He studied closely the fiery destruction of Jericho that took place—according to Kathleen Kenyon—in the middle of the 16th century B.C.E. According to him, not only did that destruction fit the Bible's account of Joshua's destruction of the city but the archaeological picture of Canaan as a whole fit perfectly with the Bible's description of

---

30. How do Bible students view archaeology?

31. What new suggestion has recently been put forward regarding the fall of Jericho?

Canaan when the Israelites invaded. Hence, he suggests that the archaeological dating is wrong and proposes that this destruction really took place in the middle of the 15th century B.C.E., during Joshua's lifetime.[21]

The Bible Is Genuine History

32 This illustrates the fact that archaeologists often differ among themselves. It is not, then, surprising that some disagree with the Bible while others agree with it. Nevertheless, some scholars are coming to respect the historicity of the Bible in general, if not in every detail. William Foxwell Albright represented one school of thought when he wrote: "There has been a general return to appreciation of the accuracy, both in general sweep and in factual detail, of the religious history of Israel. . . . To sum up, we can now again treat the Bible from beginning to end as an authentic document of religious history."[22]

Unlike ancient secular histories, the Bible frankly records the human failings of respected figures such as Moses and David

33 In fact, the Bible in itself bears the stamp of accurate history. Events are linked to specific times and dates, unlike those of most ancient myths and legends. Many events recorded in the Bible are supported by inscriptions dating from those times. Where there is a difference between

---

32. What tendency has been observed among some scholars?

33, 34. How do the Hebrew Scriptures themselves give evidence of being historically accurate?

the Bible and some ancient inscription, the discrepancy can often be attributed to the ancient rulers' distaste for recording their own defeats and their desire to magnify their successes.

34 Indeed, many of those ancient inscriptions are not history as much as they are official propaganda. In contrast, the Bible writers display a rare frankness. Major ancestral figures such as Moses and Aaron are revealed with all their weaknesses and strengths. Even the failings of the great king David are honestly revealed. The shortcomings of the nation as a whole are repeatedly exposed. This candor recommends the Hebrew Scriptures as truthful and reliable and lends weight to the words of Jesus, who, when praying to God, said: "Your word is truth."—John 17:17.

35 Albright went on to say: "In any case the Bible towers in content above all earlier religious literature; and it towers just as impressively over all subsequent literature in the direct simplicity of its message and the catholicity [comprehensive range] of its appeal to men of all lands and times."[23] It is this 'towering message,' rather than the testimony of scholars, that proves the inspiration of the Bible, as we will see in later chapters. But let us note here that modern rationalistic thinkers have failed to prove that the Hebrew Scriptures are not true history, while these writings themselves give every evidence of being accurate. Can the same be said for the Christian Greek Scriptures, the "New Testament"? We will consider this in the next chapter.

---

35. What have rationalistic thinkers failed to do, and what do Bible students look to in order to prove the inspiration of the Bible?

Chapter 5

The "New Testament"—History or Myth?

"The New Testament can be described today as the best-investigated book in world literature." So said Hans Küng in his book "On Being a Christian." And he was right. Over the past 300 years, the Christian Greek Scriptures have been more than investigated. They have been more thoroughly dissected and more minutely analyzed than any other literature.

THE conclusions reached by some investigators have been bizarre. Back in the 19th century, Ludwig Noack in Germany concluded that the Gospel of John was written in 60 C.E. by the beloved disciple—who, according to Noack, was Judas! The Frenchman Joseph Ernest Renan suggested that the resurrection of Lazarus was likely a fraud arranged by Lazarus himself to support Jesus' claim of being a miracle worker, while the German theologian Gustav Volkmar insisted that the historical Jesus could not possibly have come forward with Messianic claims.[1]

2 Bruno Bauer, on the other hand, decided that Jesus never existed at all! "He maintained that the

1, 2. (Include introduction.) (a) To what treatment have the Christian Greek Scriptures been subjected over the past 300 years? (b) What strange conclusions have been reached by some investigators?

real creative forces in early Christianity were Philo, Seneca, and the Gnostics. In the end he declared that there never had been a historical Jesus . . . that the genesis of the Christian religion was late in the second century and was from a Judaism in which Stoicism had become dominant."[2]

[3] Today, few hold such extreme ideas. But if you

3. What opinion about the Bible do many still hold?

Modern Criticism Found Wanting

As an example of the uncertain nature of modern Bible criticism, consider these remarks by Raymond E. Brown about the Gospel of John: "At the end of the last century and in the early years of this century, scholarship went through a period of extreme skepticism about this Gospel. John was dated very late, even to the second half of the 2nd century. As a product of the Hellenistic world, it was thought to be totally devoid of historical value and to have little relation to the Palestine of Jesus of Nazareth . . .

"There is not one such position that has not been affected by a series of unexpected archaeological, documentary, and textual discoveries. These discoveries have led us to challenge intelligently the critical views that had almost become orthodox and to recognize how fragile was the base which supported the highly skeptical analysis of John. . . .

"The dating of the Gospel has been moved back to the end of the 1st century or even earlier. . . . Perhaps strangest of all, some scholars are even daring to suggest once more that John the son of Zebedee may have had something to do with the Gospel"![3]

Why should it seem strange to believe that John wrote the book traditionally credited to him? Only because it does not fit in with the critics' preconceived ideas.

read the works of modern scholars, you will find many still believe that the Christian Greek Scriptures contain legend, myth, and exaggeration. Is this true?

When Were They Written?

4 It takes time for myths and legends to develop. So the question, When were these books written?, is important. Michael Grant, a historian, says that the historical writings of the Christian Greek Scriptures were begun "thirty or forty years after Jesus' death."[4] Biblical archaeologist William Foxwell Albright cited C. C. Torrey as concluding "that all the Gospels were written before 70 A.D. and that there is nothing in them which could not have been written within twenty years of the Crucifixion." Albright's own opinion was that their writing was completed "not later than about 80 A.D." Others come up with slightly different estimates, but most agree that the writing of the "New Testament" was completed by the end of the first century.

5 What does this mean? Albright concludes: "All we can say is that a period of between twenty and fifty years is too slight to permit of any appreciable corruption of the essential content and even of the specific wording of the sayings of Jesus."[5] Professor Gary Habermas adds: "The Gospels are quite close to the period of time which they record, while ancient histories often describe events which took

---

4. (a) Why is it important to know when the books of the Christian Greek Scriptures were written? (b) What are some opinions about the time of writing of the Christian Greek Scriptures?

5, 6. What should we conclude from the fact that the Christian Greek Scriptures were written not too long after the events they record?

place centuries earlier. Yet, modern historians are able to successfully derive the events even from these ancient periods of time."[6]

6 In other words, the historical parts of the Christian Greek Scriptures are worthy of at least as much credence as secular histories. Certainly, in the few decades between the events of early Christianity and their being recorded in writing, there was no time for myths and legends to develop and be universally accepted.

Eyewitness Testimony

7 This is especially true in view of the fact that many of the accounts speak of eyewitness testimony. The writer of the Gospel of John said: "This is the disciple [the disciple that Jesus loved] that bears witness about these things and that wrote these things." (John 21:24) The writer of the book of Luke says: "Those who from the beginning became eyewitnesses and attendants of the message delivered these to us." (Luke 1:2) The apostle Paul, speaking of those who witnessed the resurrection of Jesus, said: "Most of [them] remain to the present, but some have fallen asleep in death."—1 Corinthians 15:6.

8 In this connection, Professor F. F. Bruce makes a keen observation: "It can have been by no means so easy as some writers seem to think to invent words and deeds of Jesus in those early years, when so many of His disciples were about, who could remember what had and had not hap-

---

7, 8. (a) Who were still alive while the Christian Greek Scriptures were being written and circulated? (b) What must we conclude in line with the comment of Professor F. F. Bruce?

pened. . . . The disciples could not afford to risk inaccuracies (not to speak of willful manipulation of the facts), which would at once be exposed by those who would be only too glad to do so. On the contrary, one of the strong points in the original apostolic preaching is the confident appeal to the knowledge of the hearers; they not only said, 'We are witnesses of these things,' but also, 'As you yourselves also know' (Acts 2:22)."[7]

Is the Text Trustworthy?

[9] Is it possible that these eyewitness testimonies were accurately recorded but later corrupted? In other words, were myths and legends introduced after the original writing was completed? We have already seen that the text of the Christian Greek Scriptures is in better condition than any other ancient literature. Kurt and Barbara Aland, scholars of the Greek text of the Bible, list almost 5,000 manuscripts that have survived from antiquity down to today, some from as early as the second century C.E.[8] The general testimony of this mass of evidence is that the text is essentially sound. Additionally, there are many ancient translations—the earliest dating to about the year 180 C.E.—that help to prove that the text is accurate.[9]

[10] Hence, by any reckoning, we can be sure that legends and myths did not infiltrate into the Christian Greek Scriptures after the original writers finished their work. The text we have is substantially the same as the one that the original writers

---

9, 10. As far as the Christian Greek Scriptures are concerned, of what can we be certain?

penned, and its accuracy is confirmed by the fact that contemporaneous Christians accepted it. Can we, then, check the historicity of the Bible by comparing it with other ancient histories? To some extent, yes.

The Documentary Evidence

11 In fact, for events in the lives of Jesus and his apostles, documentary evidence apart from the Bible is quite limited. This is only to be expected, since in the first century, Christians were a relatively small group that did not get involved in politics. But the evidence that secular history does provide agrees with what we read in the Bible.

12 For example, after Herod Antipas suffered a resounding military defeat, the Jewish historian Josephus, writing in 93 C.E., said: "To some of the Jews the destruction of Herod's army seemed to be divine vengeance, and certainly a just vengeance, for his treatment of John, surnamed the Baptist. For Herod had put him to death, though he was a good man and had exhorted the Jews to lead righteous lives, to practise justice towards their fellows and piety towards God."[10] Thus Josephus confirms the Bible account that John the Baptizer was a righteous man who preached repentance and who was executed by Herod.—Matthew 3:1-12; 14:11.

13 Josephus also mentions James, the half brother of Jesus, who, the Bible tells us, did not initially

---

11. To what extent does external documentary evidence support the historical accounts in the Christian Greek Scriptures?

12. What does Josephus tell us about John the Baptizer?

13. How does Josephus support the historicity of James and of Jesus himself?

follow Jesus but later became a prominent elder in Jerusalem. (John 7:3-5; Galatians 1:18, 19) He documents James' arrest in these words: "[The high priest Ananus] convened the judges of the Sanhedrin and brought before them a man named James, the brother of Jesus who was called the Christ, and certain others."[11] In writing these words, Josephus additionally confirms that "Jesus, who was called the Christ" was a real, historical person.

14 Other early writers too refer to things mentioned in the Greek Scriptures. For example, the Gospels tell us that Jesus' preaching around Palestine met with a wide response. When he was sentenced to death by Pontius Pilate, his followers were confused and disheartened. Soon afterward, these same disciples boldly filled Jerusalem with the message that their Lord had been resurrected. In a few years, Christianity had spread throughout the Roman Empire.—Matthew 4:25; 26:31; 27:24-26; Acts 2:23, 24, 36; 5:28; 17:6.

15 Witness to the truth of this comes from the Roman historian Tacitus, who was no friend of Christianity. Writing soon after 100 C.E., he tells of Nero's cruel persecution of the Christians and adds: "Christus, the founder of the name, had undergone the death penalty in the reign of Tiberius, by sentence of the procurator Pontius Pilatus, and the pernicious superstition was checked for a moment, only to break out once more, not merely in Judaea, the home of the disease, but in the capital [Rome] itself."[12]

14, 15. What support does Tacitus give to the Bible record?

This altar in Pergamum was apparently dedicated "to unknown gods"

[16] At Acts 18:2 the Bible writer refers to the fact that "[the Roman emperor] Claudius had ordered all the Jews to depart from Rome." Second-century Roman historian Suetonius also refers to this expulsion. In his work *The Deified Claudius,* the historian says: "Since the Jews constantly made disturbances at the instigation of Chrestus, he [Claudius] expelled them from Rome."[13] If Chrestus here refers to Jesus Christ and if the events in Rome followed the pattern in other cities, then the riots were not actually at the instigation of Christ (that is, Christ's followers). Rather, they were the Jews' violent response to the faithful preaching activity of Christians.

[17] Justin Martyr, writing in the middle of the second century, wrote in reference to the death of Jesus: "That these things did happen, you can ascertain from the Acts of Pontius Pilate."[14] In addition, according to Justin Martyr, these same records mentioned Jesus' miracles, regarding which he says: "That He did those things, you can learn

---

16. What historical event referred to in the Bible is also referred to by Suetonius?
17. What sources that were available to Justin Martyr in the second century supported the Bible account of Jesus' miracles and his death?

from the Acts of Pontius Pilate."[15] True, these "Acts," or official records, no longer exist. But they evidently did exist in the second century, and Justin Martyr confidently challenged his readers to check them to verify the truth of what he said.

The Archaeological Evidence

18 Archaeological discoveries have also illustrated or confirmed what we read in the Greek Scriptures. Thus, in 1961 the name of Pontius Pilate was found in an inscription in the ruins of a Roman theater at Caesarea.[16] Until this discovery, there had been only limited evidence, apart from the Bible itself, of the existence of this Roman ruler.

19 In Luke's Gospel, we read that John the Baptizer began his ministry "when . . . Lysanias was district ruler of Abilene." (Luke 3:1) Some doubted that statement because Josephus mentioned a Lysanias who ruled Abilene and who died in 34 B.C.E., long before the birth of John. However, archaeologists have uncovered an inscription in Abilene mentioning another Lysanias who was tetrarch

18. What support does archaeology give to the existence of Pontius Pilate?
19, 20. What Bible personalities mentioned by Luke (in Luke and Acts) have been attested to by archaeology?

Ruins of the once magnificent temple of Artemis of which the Ephesians were so proud

The Bible honestly reports that Peter denied knowing Jesus

(district ruler) during the reign of Tiberius, who was ruling as Caesar in Rome when John began his ministry.[17] This could easily have been the Lysanias to whom Luke was referring.

20 In Acts we read that Paul and Barnabas were sent to do missionary work in Cyprus and there met up with a proconsul named Sergius Paulus, "an intelligent man." (Acts 13:7) In the middle of the 19th century, excavations in Cyprus uncovered an inscription dating from 55 C.E. that mentions this very man. Of this, archaeologist G. Ernest Wright says: "It is the one reference we have to this proconsul outside the Bible and it is interesting that Luke gives us correctly his name and title."[18]

21 When he was in Athens, Paul said he had observed an altar that was dedicated "To an Unknown God." (Acts 17:23) Altars dedicated in Latin to anonymous gods have been discovered in parts of the territory of the Roman Empire. One was found in Pergamum with the inscription written in Greek, as would have been the case in Athens.

22 Later, while in Ephesus, Paul was violently opposed by silversmiths, whose income was derived

---

21, 22. What religious practices of Bible record have been confirmed by archaeological discoveries?

from making shrines and images of the goddess Artemis. Ephesus was referred to as "the temple keeper of the great Artemis." (Acts 19:35) In harmony with this, a number of terra-cotta and marble figurines of Artemis have been discovered at the site of ancient Ephesus. During the last century, the remains of the huge temple itself were excavated.

The Ring of Truth

23 Hence, history and archaeology illustrate, and to some extent confirm, the historical elements of the Greek Scriptures. But, again, the strongest proof of the truth of these writings is in the books themselves. When you read them, they do not sound like myths. They have the ring of truth.

24 For one thing, they are very frank. Think of what is recorded about Peter. His embarrassing failure to walk on water is detailed. Then, Jesus says to this highly respected apostle: "Get behind me, Satan!" (Matthew 14:28-31; 16:23) Moreover, after vigorously protesting that even if all the others abandoned Jesus, *he* would never do so, Peter fell asleep on his night watch and then denied his Lord three times.—Matthew 26:31-35, 37-45, 73-75.

25 But Peter is not the only one whose weaknesses are exposed. The frank record does not gloss over the apostles' bickering about who was the greatest among them. (Matthew 18:1; Mark 9:34;

23, 24. (a) Where do we find the strongest proof of the truth of the writings of the Christian Greek Scriptures? (b) What quality inherent in the Bible record testifies to its truthfulness? Illustrate.

25. What weaknesses of the apostles do Bible writers frankly expose?

Luke 22:24) Nor does it omit telling us that the mother of the apostles James and John asked Jesus to give her sons the most favored positions in his Kingdom. (Matthew 20:20-23) The "sharp burst of anger" between Barnabas and Paul is also faithfully documented.—Acts 15:36-39.

26 Noteworthy, too, is the fact that the book of Luke tells us that it was "the women, who had come with him out of Galilee," who first learned about Jesus' resurrection. This is a most unusual detail in the male-dominated society of the first century. Indeed, according to the record, what the women were saying "appeared as nonsense" to the apostles. (Luke 23:55–24:11) If the history in the Greek Scriptures is not true, it must have been invented. But why would anyone invent a story portraying such respected figures in such an unflattering light? These details would have been included only if they were true.

Why would the Bible report that Jesus' resurrection was first discovered by women if this did not really happen?

Jesus—A Real Person

27 Many have viewed Jesus as he is described in the Bible as an idealized fiction. But historian Michael Grant notes: "If we apply to the New Testament, as we should, the same sort of criteria as we

26. What detail about Jesus' resurrection would have been included only if it was true?
27. How does one historian testify to the historical existence of Jesus?

The Bible candidly records the "sharp burst of anger" between Paul and Barnabas

should apply to other ancient writings containing historical material, we can no more reject Jesus' existence than we can reject the existence of a mass of pagan personages whose reality as historical figures is never questioned."[19]

28 Not only Jesus' existence but also his personality comes through in the Bible with a decided ring of truth. It is not easy to invent an unusual character and then present a consistent portrait of him throughout a whole book. It is nearly impossible for four different writers to write about the same character and consistently paint the same picture of him if that character never really existed. The fact that the Jesus described in all four Gospels is obviously the same person is persuasive evidence of the Gospels' truthfulness.

29 Michael Grant quotes a very appropriate question: "How comes it that, through all the Gospel traditions without exception, there comes a remarkably firmly-drawn portrait of an attractive young man moving freely about among women of all sorts, including the decidedly disreputable,

---

28, 29. Why is it significant that the four Gospels present a unified picture of Jesus' personality?

without a trace of sentimentality, unnaturalness, or prudery, and yet, at every point, maintaining a simple integrity of character?"[20] The only answer is that such a man really existed and acted in the way the Bible says.

Why They Do Not Believe

30 Since there is compelling evidence for saying that the Greek Scriptures are true history, why do some say they are not? Why is it that many, while accepting parts of them as genuine, nevertheless refuse to accept everything they contain? It is mainly because the Bible records things that modern intellectuals do not want to believe. It tells, for example, that Jesus both fulfilled and uttered prophecies. It also tells that he performed miracles and that after his death he was resurrected.

31 In this skeptical 20th century, such things are incredible. Regarding miracles, Professor Ezra P. Gould notes: "There is one reservation which some of the critics feel themselves justified in making . . . *that miracles do not happen.*"[21] Some accept that Jesus may have effected healings, but only of the psychosomatic, 'mind over matter,' type. As for

30, 31. Why do many not accept the Christian Greek Scriptures as historically accurate despite all the evidence?

The consistency of the portrayal of Jesus in the four Gospels is a strong proof of their genuineness

Most modern critics take it for granted that miracles do not happen

the other miracles, most explain them away either as inventions or as real events that were distorted in the telling.

32 As an example of this, consider the occasion when Jesus fed a crowd of more than 5,000 with just a few loaves and two fishes. (Matthew 14:14-22) Nineteenth-century scholar Heinrich Paulus suggested that what really happened was this: Jesus and his apostles found themselves attended by a large multitude that were getting hungry. So he decided to set a good example for the rich among them. He took what little food he and his apostles had and shared it with the multitude. Soon, others who had brought food followed his example and shared theirs. Finally, the whole multitude was fed.[22]

33 If this is what really happened, though, it was a remarkable proof of the power of good example. Why would such an interesting and meaningful story be distorted to make it sound like a supernatural miracle? Indeed, all such efforts to explain away the miracles as other than miraculous pose more

32, 33. How have some tried to explain away Jesus' miracle of feeding the large crowd, but why is this illogical?

problems than they solve. And they are all based on a false premise. They start by *assuming* that miracles are impossible. But why should that be the case?

[34] According to the most reasonable standards, both the Hebrew and the Greek Scriptures are genuine history, yet they both contain examples of prophecy and miracles. (Compare 2 Kings 4:42-44.) What, then, if the prophecies are genuine? And what if miracles actually did occur? Then God was indeed behind the writing of the Bible, and it really is his word, not man's. In a future chapter, we will discuss the question of prophecy, but first let us consider miracles. Is it reasonable in this 20th century to believe that in earlier centuries miracles did happen?

34. If the Bible really does contain accurate prophecy and accounts of genuine miracles, what does this prove?

Just Another Attack on the Bible

Timothy P. Weber writes: "The findings of higher criticism forced many lay people to doubt their ability to understand anything [in the Bible]. . . . A. T. Pierson expressed the frustration of many evangelicals when he stated that 'like Romanism, [higher criticism] practically removes the Word of God from the common people by assuming that only scholars can interpret it; while Rome puts a priest between a man and the Word, criticism puts an educated expositor between the believer and his Bible.'"[23] Thus, modern higher criticism is exposed as just another attack on the Bible.

Chapter 6

The Miracles—Did They Really Happen?

One day in 31 C.E., Jesus and his disciples were traveling to Nain, a city in northern Palestine. As they got close to the gate of the city, they met up with a funeral procession. The deceased was a young man. His mother was a widow, and he had been her only son, so now she was all alone. According to the record, Jesus "was moved with pity for her, and he said to her: 'Stop weeping.' With that he approached and touched the bier, and the bearers stood still, and he said: 'Young man, I say to you, Get up!' And the dead man sat up and started to speak."—Luke 7:11-15.

IT IS a heartwarming story, but is it true? Many find it hard to believe that such things ever really happened. Nevertheless, miracles are an integral part of the Bible record. Belief in the Bible means believing that miracles occurred. In fact, the whole pattern of Bible truth depends on one very important miracle: the resurrection of Jesus Christ.

Why Some Do Not Believe

2 Do you believe in miracles? Or do you feel

---

1. (Include introduction.) (a) What miracle did Jesus perform near the city of Nain? (b) How important are miracles in the Bible, yet do all people believe that they really happened?

2, 3. What is one line of reasoning that the Scottish philosopher David Hume used in an effort to prove that miracles do not happen?

that in this scientific age, it is illogical to believe in miracles—that is, in extraordinary events that give evidence of superhuman intervention? If you do not believe, you are not the first. Two centuries ago, the Scottish philosopher David Hume had the same problem. It may be that your reasons for disbelief are similar to his.

3 Hume's objections to the idea of miracles included three outstanding points.[1] First, he writes: "A miracle is a violation of the laws of nature." Man has relied from time immemorial on the laws of nature. He has known that an object will fall if it is dropped, that the sun will rise each morning and set each night, and so forth. Instinctively, he knows that events will always follow such familiar patterns. Nothing will ever happen that is out of harmony with natural laws. This 'proof,' Hume felt, "is as entire as any argument from experience" against the possibility of miracles.

4 A second argument he presented was that people are easily fooled. Some *want* to believe in marvels and miracles, especially when it has to do with religion, and many so-called miracles have turned out to be fakes. A third argument was that miracles are usually reported in times of ignorance. The more educated people become, the fewer miracles are reported. As Hume expressed it, "Such prodigious events never happen in our days." Thus, he felt it proved that they never did happen.

5 To this day, most arguments against miracles

4, 5. What are two other reasons put forward by David Hume to disclaim the possibility of miracles?

follow these general principles, so let us consider Hume's objections, one by one.

Against the Laws of Nature?

6 What about the objection that miracles are 'violations of the laws of nature' and therefore cannot be true? On the surface, this might seem persuasive; but analyze what is really being said. Usually, a miracle can be defined as something that occurs outside the normal laws of nature.* It is an occurrence so unexpected that onlookers are convinced they have witnessed superhuman intervention. Hence, what the objection really means is: 'Miracles are impossible because they are miraculous!' Why not consider the evidence before jumping to such a conclusion?

7 The truth is, educated people today are less prepared than was David Hume to insist that the familiar laws of nature hold true everywhere and at all times. Scientists are willing to speculate on whether, instead of the familiar three dimensions of length, breadth, and height, there may be many additional dimensions in the universe.[2] They theorize on the existence of black holes, huge stars that collapse in on themselves until their density is

---

* We say "usually," because some miracles in the Bible may have involved natural phenomena, such as earthquakes or landslides. They are still viewed as miracles, however, because they happened exactly at the time they were needed and thus were evidently at God's direction.—Joshua 3:15, 16; 6:20.

---

6. Why is it illogical to object to the idea of miracles on the ground that they are 'violations of the laws of nature'?
7, 8. (a) With respect to the laws of nature as we know them, in what ways have scientists become more broad-minded in their view of what is and is not possible? (b) If we believe in God, what should we also believe as to his capacity to do unusual things?

virtually infinite. In their vicinity the fabric of space is said to be so distorted that time itself stands still.[3] Scientists have even debated whether, under certain conditions, time would run backward instead of forward![4]

[8] Stephen W. Hawking, Lucasian Professor of Mathematics at Cambridge University, when discussing how the universe began, said: "In the classical theory of general relativity . . . the beginning of the universe has to be a singularity of infinite density and space-time curvature. Under such conditions, all the known laws of physics would break down."[5] So, modern scientists do not agree that because something is contrary to the normal laws of nature it can never happen. In unusual conditions, unusual things *may* happen. Surely, if we believe in an almighty God, we should admit that he has the power to cause unusual—miraculous—events to take place when it befits his purpose.—Exodus 15:6-10; Isaiah 40:13, 15.

What About the Fakes?

[9] No reasonable person would deny that there are fake miracles. For example, some claim the power to heal the sick by miraculous faith healing. A medical doctor, William A. Nolan, made it his special project to investigate such healings. He followed up on numerous claimed cures among both evangelical faith healers in the United States and so-called psychic surgeons in Asia. The result? All he found were examples of disappointment and fraud.[6]

---

9. Is it true that some miracles are fakes? Explain your answer.

Many view the reliability of the laws of nature, such as the fact that the sun rises every morning, as proof that miracles cannot happen

10 Do such frauds mean that genuine miracles never happened? Not necessarily. Sometimes we hear of forged bank notes being put into circulation, but that does not mean that all money is forged. Some sick people put a lot of faith in quacks, fraudulent doctors, and give a lot of money to them. But that does not mean that all doctors are fraudulent. Some artists have been skilled at forging "old master" paintings. But that does not mean that all paintings are fakes. Neither does the fact that some claimed miracles are clearly fakes mean that genuine miracles can never happen.

'Miracles Do Not Happen Now'

11 The third objection was summed up in the expression: "Such prodigious events never happen in our days." Hume had never seen a miracle, so he refused to believe that miracles could happen. This kind of reasoning, however, is inconsistent. Any thinking person has to admit that, before the days of the Scottish philosopher, "prodigious events" happened that were not repeated during his lifetime. What events?

---

10. Do you feel that the fact that some miracles have been demonstrated to be fake proves that all miracles are fraudulent?
11. What was David Hume's third objection to the idea of miracles?

[12] For one thing, life began on earth. Then, certain forms of life were endowed with consciousness. Eventually, man appeared, endowed with wisdom, imagination, the capacity to love, and the faculty of conscience. No scientist can explain on the basis of the laws of nature that operate today how such extraordinary things happened. Yet we have living evidence that they did happen.

[13] And what about "prodigious events" that have happened since David Hume's day? Suppose we were able to travel back in time and tell him about today's world. Imagine trying to explain that a businessman in Hamburg can speak to someone thousands of miles away in Tokyo without even raising his voice; that a soccer match in Spain can be seen all around the earth *even as it is being played;* that vessels much larger than the oceangoing ships of Hume's day can rise from the surface of the earth and carry 500 people through the air for thousands of miles in a matter of hours. Can you imagine his response? 'Impossible! Such prodigious events never happen in our days!'

[14] Yet such 'prodigies' do happen in *our* days. Why? Because man, using scientific principles of which Hume had no concept, has learned to construct telephones, television sets, and airplanes. Is it, then, so difficult to believe that on occasion in the past God could have, in ways that we still do

---

12. What wonderful events happened in the past that cannot be explained by the laws of nature that operate today?

13, 14. What things are commonplace today that would have seemed miraculous to David Hume?

not understand, accomplished things that to us are miraculous?

How Can We Know?

15 Of course, saying that miracles *could* have happened does not mean that they did. How can we know, in this 20th century, whether back in Bible times God worked genuine miracles through his servants on earth or not? What kind of evidence would you expect for such things? Imagine a primitive tribesman who has been taken from his jungle home to visit a big city. When he returns, how can he describe to his people the wonders of civilization? He cannot explain how an automobile works or why music comes out of a portable radio. He cannot build a computer to prove that such a thing exists. All he can do is tell what he has seen.

16 We are in the same situation as that man's fellow tribesmen. If God really has worked miracles, the only way we can learn about them is from eyewitnesses. The eyewitnesses cannot explain how the miracles happened, nor can they duplicate them. They can only tell us what they saw. Obviously, eyewitnesses can be duped. They can also easily exaggerate and misinform. If, then, we are

15, 16. If miracles really did happen, what is the only way we could know about them? Illustrate your answer.

The creation of the earth as a home for living things was a 'prodigious event' that was not repeated

How would you explain the marvels of modern science to someone living 200 years ago?

to believe their testimony, we need to know that these eyewitnesses are truthful, are of high quality, and have proved that they have good motives.

The Best-Attested Miracle

17 The best-attested miracle in the Bible is the resurrection of Jesus Christ, so why not use this as a test case, so to speak. First, consider the reported facts: Jesus was arrested on the evening of Nisan 14—which happened to be a Thursday night in our modern way of reckoning the week.* He appeared before the leaders of the Jews who accused him of blasphemy and decided he had to die. The Jewish leaders led Jesus before the Roman governor Pontius Pilate, who succumbed to their pressure and handed him over for execution. On Friday afternoon—still Nisan 14 on the Jewish calendar—he was nailed to a torture stake and in a few hours was dead.—Mark 14:43-65; 15:1-39.

18 After a Roman soldier pierced Jesus' side with

* The Jewish day began at about six in the evening and continued until six the following evening.

17. (a) What is the best-attested miracle in the Bible? (b) What were the circumstances that led up to Jesus' death?
18. According to the Bible, how did the report of Jesus' resurrection begin to circulate?

a spear to make sure he was really dead, Jesus' body was buried in a new tomb. The following day, Nisan 15 (Friday/Saturday), was a sabbath. But on the morning of Nisan 16—Sunday morning—some disciples went to the tomb and found it empty. Soon, stories began to circulate that Jesus had been seen alive. The initial reaction to these stories was exactly what it would be today—disbelief. Even the apostles refused to believe. But when they themselves saw the living Jesus, they had no choice but to accept that he had indeed been raised from the dead.—John 19:31–20:29; Luke 24:11.

The Empty Tomb

19 Had Jesus been resurrected, or is all this just a fabrication? One thing that people back then would likely have asked is: Is Jesus' body still in his tomb? Jesus' followers would have faced a huge obstacle if their opponents could have pointed to his actual corpse still in its burial place as evidence that he had not been resurrected. There is, however, no record that they ever did this. Rather, according to the Bible, they gave money to the soldiers assigned to guard the tomb and told them: "Say, 'His disciples came in the night and stole him while we were sleeping.'" (Matthew 28:11-13) We also have evidence outside the Bible that the Jewish leaders acted in this way.

20 About a century after Jesus' death, Justin Martyr wrote a work called *Dialogue With Trypho*. In this, he said: "You [the Jews] have sent chosen

---

19-21. (a) According to Justin Martyr, how did the Jews counter the preaching by Christians about Jesus' resurrection? (b) What can we be sure was true about Jesus' tomb on Nisan 16?

and ordained men throughout all the world to proclaim that a godless and lawless heresy had sprung from one Jesus, a Galilæan deceiver, whom we crucified, but his disciples stole him by night from the tomb, where he was laid."[7]

21 Now, Trypho was a Jew, and the *Dialogue With Trypho* was written to defend Christianity against Judaism. Hence, it is unlikely that Justin Martyr would have said what he did—that the Jews accused the Christians of stealing Jesus' body from the tomb—if the Jews had not made such a charge. Otherwise, he would have left himself open to an easily verifiable charge of lying. Justin Martyr would have said this only if the Jews really had sent out such messengers. And they would have done so only if the tomb really was empty on Nisan 16, 33 C.E. and if they could not point to Jesus' body in the tomb as evidence that he had not been resurrected. So since the tomb was empty, what had happened? *Did* the disciples steal the body? Or was it removed miraculously as evidence that Jesus had really been resurrected?

The Conclusion of Luke the Physician

22 One highly educated man of the first century who carefully considered the evidence was Luke, a physician. (Colossians 4:14) Luke wrote two books that are now a part of the Bible: one was a Gospel, or history of Jesus' ministry, and the other, called the Acts of Apostles, was a history of the spread of Christianity in the years following Jesus' death.

22, 23. Who was one educated man of the first century who looked into the resurrection of Jesus, and what sources of information were available to him?

23 In the introduction to his Gospel, Luke refers to much evidence that was available to him but that is no longer available to us. He speaks of the written documents about Jesus' life that he consulted. He also notes that he spoke with eyewitnesses of Jesus' life, death, and resurrection. Then, he says: "I have traced all things from the start with accuracy." (Luke 1:1-3) Evidently, Luke's research was thorough. Was he a good historian?

Christianity's enemies said that the disciples stole Jesus' body. If this were the case, why would Christians have been willing to die for a faith based on his resurrection?

24 Many have attested that he was. Back in 1913, Sir William Ramsay in a lecture commented on the historicity of the works of Luke. His conclusion? "Luke is a historian of the first rank; not merely are his statements of fact trustworthy; he is possessed of the true historic sense."[8] More recent researchers have come to the same conclusion. *The Living Word Commentary,* when introducing its volumes on Luke, says: "Luke was both a historian (and an accurate one) and a theologian."

25 Dr. David Gooding, a former professor of Old Testament Greek in Northern Ireland, declares that Luke was "an ancient historian in the tradition of the Old Testament historians and in the tradition of Thucydides [one of the highest-rated

24, 25. How do many view Luke's qualifications as a historian?

historians of the ancient world]. Like them he will have taken great pains in investigating his sources, in selecting his material, and in disposing that material. . . . Thucydides combined this method with a passion for historical accuracy: there is no reason for thinking that Luke did less."[9]

26 What was the conclusion of this highly qualified man about why Jesus' tomb was empty on Nisan 16? Both in his Gospel and in the book of Acts, Luke reports as a fact that Jesus was raised from the dead. (Luke 24:1-52; Acts 1:3) He had no doubt at all about it. Perhaps his belief in the miracle of the resurrection was strengthened by his own experiences. While he was not apparently an eyewitness of the resurrection, he does report witnessing miracles that were performed by the apostle Paul.—Acts 14:8-10; 20:7-12; 28:8, 9.

They Saw the Resurrected Jesus

27 Two of the Gospels are traditionally ascribed to men who knew Jesus, saw him die, and claimed to have actually seen him after his resurrection. These are the apostle Matthew, the former tax collector, and John, Jesus' beloved apostle. Another Bible writer, the apostle Paul, also claimed to have seen the risen Christ. Paul, in addition, lists by name others who saw Jesus alive after his death, and he says that at one time Jesus appeared to "upward of five hundred brothers."—1 Corinthians 15:3-8.

---

26. (a) What was Luke's conclusion regarding Jesus' resurrection? (b) What may have strengthened him in this conclusion?

27. Who are some who claimed to have seen the resurrected Jesus?

[28] One whom Paul mentions as an eyewitness is James, Jesus' fleshly half brother, who must have known Jesus since childhood. Another is the apostle Peter; the historian Luke reports that he gave a fearless witness about Jesus' resurrection just a few weeks after Jesus' death. (Acts 2:23, 24) Two letters in the Bible are traditionally ascribed to Peter, and in the first of these Peter shows that his belief in the resurrection of Jesus was still a powerful motivation even many years after the event. He wrote: "Blessed be the God and Father of our Lord Jesus Christ, for according to his great mercy he gave us a new birth to a living hope through the resurrection of Jesus Christ from the dead." —1 Peter 1:3.

[29] Hence, just as Luke could speak with people who claimed to have seen and to have spoken with Jesus after his death, we can read the words that some of these wrote. And we can judge for ourselves whether those people were deceived, whether they were trying to deceive us, or whether they really did see the resurrected Christ. Frankly, there is no way that they could have been deceived. A number of them were Jesus' intimate friends up until his death. Some of them witnessed his agony on the torture stake. They saw the blood and water flow out from the spear wound inflicted by the soldier. The soldier knew, and they knew, that Jesus was indisputably dead. Later, they say, they saw Jesus alive and actually spoke with him. No, they

---

28. What effect did the resurrection of Jesus have on Peter?
29. Although we cannot speak with eyewitnesses of the resurrection, what impressive evidence is nevertheless available to us?

could not have been deceived. Were they, then, trying to deceive us in saying that Jesus had been resurrected?—John 19:32-35; 21:4, 15-24.

30 To answer this, we have merely to ask ourselves: Did they themselves believe what they were saying? Yes, without any doubt. To the Christians, including those who claimed to be eyewitnesses, the resurrection of Jesus was the whole basis of their belief. The apostle Paul said: "If Christ has not been raised up, our preaching is certainly in vain, and our faith is in vain . . . If Christ has not been raised up, your faith is useless." (1 Corinthians 15:14, 17) Does that sound like the words of a man who is lying when he says he has seen the resurrected Christ?

31 Consider what it meant to be a Christian in those days. There was no gain in prestige, power, or wealth. Quite the contrary. Many of the early Christians 'joyfully took the plundering of their belongings' for the sake of their faith. (Hebrews 10: 34) Christianity called for a life of sacrifice and persecution that in many cases ended in martyrdom by a shameful, painful death.

32 Some Christians came from prosperous families, like the apostle John whose father evidently had a flourishing fishing business in Galilee. Many had good prospects, such as Paul who, when he accepted Christianity, had been a student of the famous rabbi Gamaliel and was beginning to

---

30. Why is it impossible that the early eyewitnesses of Jesus' resurrection were lying?

31, 32. What sacrifices were made by early Christians, and why is this strong evidence that these Christians were telling the truth when they said that Jesus had been resurrected?

Why No Miracles Today?

Sometimes the question is raised: 'Why are there no miracles of the Bible kind today?' The answer is that miracles served their purpose back then, but today God expects us to live by faith.—Habakkuk 2:2-4; Hebrews 10:37-39.

In the days of Moses, miracles occurred to establish Moses' credentials. They showed that Jehovah was using him and also that the Law covenant was truly of divine origin and that the Israelites were henceforth God's chosen people. —Exodus 4:1-9, 30, 31; Deuteronomy 4:33, 34.

In the first century, miracles helped to establish the credentials of Jesus and, after him, of the young Christian congregation. They helped to demonstrate that Jesus was the promised Messiah, that after his death fleshly Israel was replaced as God's special people by the Christian congregation, and thus that the Law of Moses was no longer binding. —Acts 19:11-20; Hebrews 2:3, 4.

After the days of the apostles, the time for miracles was past. The apostle Paul explained: "Whether there are gifts of prophesying, they will be done away with; whether there are tongues, they will cease; whether there is knowledge, it will be done away with. For we have partial knowledge and we prophesy partially; but when that which is complete arrives, that which is partial will be done away with."—1 Corinthians 13: 8-10.

Today, we have the complete Bible, which includes all the revelations and counsel of God. We have the fulfillment of prophecy, and we have an advanced understanding of God's purposes. Hence, there is no more need for miracles. Nevertheless, the same spirit of God that made the miracles possible still exists and produces results that give equally strong evidence of divine power. We shall see more of this in a future chapter.

distinguish himself in the eyes of the Jewish rulers. (Acts 9:1, 2; 22:3; Galatians 1:14) Yet, all turned their backs on what this world offered in order to spread a message based on the fact that Jesus had been resurrected from the dead. (Colossians 1:23, 28) Why would they make such sacrifices to suffer for a cause they *knew* was based on a lie? The answer is, they would not. They were willing to suffer and die for a cause they knew to be founded on *truth*.

Miracles Really Happen

33 Indeed, the testimonial evidence is absolutely convincing. Jesus really was raised from the dead on Nisan 16, 33 C.E. And since that resurrection happened, all the other miracles of the Bible are possible—miracles for which we also have solid, eyewitness testimony. The same Power who raised Jesus from the dead also enabled Jesus to raise the son of the widow of Nain. He also empowered Jesus to perform the lesser—but still wonderful—miracles of healing. He was behind the miraculous feeding of the multitude, and He also enabled Jesus to walk on water.—Luke 7:11-15; Matthew 11:4-6; 14:14-21, 23-31.

34 Thus, the fact that the Bible tells of miracles is no reason to doubt its truthfulness. Rather, the fact that miracles did happen in Bible times is a powerful proof that the Bible really is the Word of God. But there is another accusation made against the Bible. Many say that it contradicts itself and therefore cannot be God's Word. Is this true?

33, 34. Since the resurrection really happened, what can we say about the other miracles of the Bible?

Chapter 7

Does the Bible Contradict Itself?

A charge often made against the Bible is that it contradicts itself. Usually, people who make this charge have not personally read the Bible; they are merely repeating what they have heard. Some, though, have found what seem to be genuine contradictions and are troubled by them.

IF IT really is the Word of God, the Bible should be harmonious, not contradictory. Why, then, do some passages seem to contradict others? To answer, we need to remember that, while the Bible is the Word of God, it was written down by a number of men over a period of several centuries. These writers had different backgrounds, writing styles, and gifts, and all these differences are reflected in the writing.

2 Moreover, if two or more writers discuss the same event, one might include details that another omits. Additionally, different writers present the subject matter in different ways. One might write it down chronologically, while another might follow a different arrangement. In this chapter, we will

1, 2. (Include introduction.) (a) What charge is often made against the Bible? (b) In comparing different Bible passages, what should we remember? (c) What are some reasons why there is sometimes a difference in the way two Bible writers report the same event?

present some alleged contradictions in the Bible and consider how they can be reconciled, taking the above considerations into account.

Independent Witnesses

3 Some "contradictions" arise when we have two or more accounts of the same incident. For example, at Matthew 8:5 we read that when Jesus came into Capernaum, "an army officer came to him, entreating him," asking Jesus to cure his manservant. But at Luke 7:3, we read of this army officer that "he sent forth older men of the Jews to him to ask [Jesus] to come and bring his slave safely through." Did the army officer speak to Jesus, or did he send the older men?

4 The answer is, clearly, that the man sent the elders of the Jews. Why, then, does Matthew say that the man himself entreated Jesus? Because, in effect, the man asked Jesus through the Jewish elders. The elders served as his mouthpiece.

5 To illustrate this, at 2 Chronicles 3:1, we read: "Finally Solomon started to build the house of Jehovah in Jerusalem." Later, we read: "Thus Solomon finished the house of Jehovah." (2 Chronicles 7:11) Did Solomon personally build the temple from start to finish? Of course not. The actual building work was done by a multitude of craftsmen and laborers. But Solomon was the organizer of the work, the one responsible. Hence, the Bible

---

3, 4. Regarding the army officer whose manservant was sick, what apparent discrepancy exists between Matthew's account and that of Luke, and how can these accounts be reconciled?

5. Why does the Bible say that Solomon built the temple, when the actual work was clearly done by others?

says that he built the house. In the same way, Matthew's Gospel tells us that the military commander approached Jesus. But Luke gives the added detail that he approached him *through* the Jewish elders.

6 Here is a similar example. At Matthew 20:20, 21, we read: "The mother of the sons of Zebedee approached [Jesus] with her sons, doing obeisance and asking for something from him." What she asked was that her sons should have the most favored position when Jesus came into his Kingdom. In Mark's account of this same event, we read: "James and John, the two sons of Zebedee, stepped up to [Jesus] and said to him: 'Teacher, we want you to do for us whatever it is we ask you for.'" (Mark 10:35-37) Was it the two sons of Zebedee, or was it their mother, who made the request of Jesus?

Apparent discrepancies in the Bible prove that the writers were truly independent witnesses

7 Clearly, it was the two sons of Zebedee who made the request, as Mark states. But they made it *through* their mother. She was their spokesperson. This is supported by Matthew's report that when the other apostles heard what the mother of the sons of Zebedee had done, they became indignant, not at the mother, but "at the two brothers."—Matthew 20:24.

8 Have you ever heard two people describe an

6, 7. How can we reconcile the two different Gospel accounts of the request of the sons of Zebedee?

8. How is it possible for two different accounts of the same event to differ from each other and yet both be the truth?

event that they both witnessed? If so, did you notice that each person emphasized details that impressed him? One may have left out things that the other included. Both, however, were telling the truth. It is the same with the four Gospel accounts of Jesus' ministry, as well as with other historical events reported by more than one Bible writer. Each writer wrote accurate information even when one retained details that another omitted. By considering all the accounts, a fuller understanding of what happened can be gained. Such variations prove that the Bible accounts are independent. And their essential harmony proves that they are true.

Read the Context

9 Often, apparent inconsistencies can be resolved if we just look at the context. Consider, for example, the often-raised problem about Cain's wife. At Genesis 4:1, 2 we read: "In time [Eve] gave birth to Cain and said: 'I have produced a man with the aid of Jehovah.' Later she again gave birth, to his brother Abel." As is well known, Cain killed Abel; but after that, we read that Cain had a wife and children. (Genesis 4:17) If Adam and Eve had only two sons, where did Cain find his wife?

10 The solution lies in the fact that Adam and Eve had more than two children. According to the context, they had a large family. At Genesis 5:3 we read that Adam became father to another son named Seth and then, in the following verse, we read: "He became father to sons and daughters." (Genesis 5:4) So Cain could have married one of his

---

9, 10. In what way does the context help us to see where Cain got his wife?

sisters or even one of his nieces. At that early stage of human history, when mankind was so close to perfection, such a marriage evidently did not pose the risks for the children of the union that it would today.

Consideration of the context often helps to solve alleged contradictions

11 Our considering the context also helps us to understand what some have claimed is a disagreement between the apostle Paul and James. At Ephesians 2:8, 9, Paul says that Christians are saved by faith, not by works. He says: "You have been saved through faith . . . not owing to works." James, however, insists on the importance of works. He writes: "As the body without spirit is dead, so also faith without works is dead." (James 2:26) How can these two statements be reconciled?

12 Considering the context of Paul's words, we find that one statement complements the other. The apostle Paul is referring to the efforts of the Jews to keep the Mosaic Law. They believed that if they kept the Law in all its details, they would be righteous. Paul pointed out that this was impossible. We can never become righteous—and thus deserve salvation—by our own works, for we are inherently sinful. We can only be saved by faith in Jesus' ransom sacrifice.—Romans 5:18.

13 James, however, adds the vital point that faith in itself is valueless if not supported by actions. A

11. What alleged disagreement between James and the apostle Paul do some point to?

12, 13. How do the words of James complement rather than contradict those of the apostle Paul?

person who claims to have faith in Jesus should prove it by what he does. An inactive faith is a dead faith and will not lead to salvation.

[14] The apostle Paul was in full agreement with this, and he often mentions the kinds of works that Christians should engage in to demonstrate their faith. For example, to the Romans he wrote: "With the heart one exercises faith for righteousness, *but with the mouth one makes public declaration for salvation.*" Making a "public declaration"—sharing our faith with others—is vital for salvation. (Romans 10:10; see also 1 Corinthians 15:58; Ephesians 5:15, 21-33; 6:15; 1 Timothy 4:16; 2 Timothy 4:5; Hebrews 10:23-25.) No work, however, that a Christian can do, and certainly no effort to fulfill the Law of Moses, will *earn* him the right to everlasting life. This is "the gift God gives" to those who exercise faith.—Romans 6:23; John 3:16.

Different Viewpoints

[15] Sometimes the Bible writers wrote about the same event from different viewpoints, or they presented their accounts in different ways. When these differences are taken into consideration, further apparent contradictions are easy to resolve. An example of this is in Numbers 35:14, where Moses speaks of the territory east of the Jordan as "on this side of the Jordan." Joshua, however, speaking

---

14. In what passages does Paul show that he is in full harmony with the principle that a living faith must be demonstrated by works?

15, 16. How could both Moses and Joshua be correct when one said that east of the Jordan was "this side" of the river while the other said it was "the other side"?

"Discrepancies" Do Not Have to Be Contradictions

Kenneth S. Kantzer, a theologian, once illustrated how two reports of the same event can seem contradictory and yet both be true. He wrote: "Some time ago the mother of a dear friend of ours was killed. We first learned of her death through a trusted mutual friend who reported that our friend's mother had been standing on the street corner waiting for a bus, had been hit by another bus passing by, was fatally injured, and died a few minutes later."

Soon after, he heard a very different report. He says: "We learned from the grandson of the dead woman that she had been involved in a collision, was thrown from the car in which she was riding, and was killed instantly. The boy was quite certain of his facts.

"Much later . . . we probed for a harmonization. We learned that the grandmother had been waiting for a bus, was hit by another bus, and was critically injured. She had been picked up by a passing car and dashed to the hospital, but in the haste, the car in which she was being transported to the hospital collided with another car. She was thrown from the car and died instantly."

Yes, two accounts of the same event may both be true even though they seem to disagree with each other. This is sometimes the case with the Bible. Independent witnesses may describe different details about the same event. Instead of being contradictory, however, what they write is complementary, and if we take all accounts into consideration, we get a better understanding of what happened.

of land to the east of the Jordan, called it "the other side of the Jordan." (Joshua 22:4) Which is correct?

[16] In fact, both are correct. According to the account in Numbers, the Israelites had not yet crossed the Jordan River into the Promised Land, so to them east of the Jordan was "this side." But Joshua had already crossed the Jordan. He was now, physically, west of the river, in the land of Canaan. So east of the Jordan was, for him, "the other side."

[17] Additionally, the way a narrative is constructed can lead to an apparent contradiction. At Genesis 1:24-26, the Bible indicates that the animals were created before man. But at Genesis 2:7, 19, 20, it seems to say that man was created before the animals. Why the discrepancy? Because the two accounts of the creation discuss it from two different viewpoints. The first describes the creation of the heavens and the earth and everything in them. (Genesis 1:1–2:4) The second concentrates on the creation of the human race and its fall into sin.—Genesis 2:5–4:26.

[18] The first account is constructed chronologically, divided into six consecutive "days." The second is written in order of topical importance. After a short prologue, it logically goes straight to the creation of Adam, since he and his family are the subject of what follows. (Genesis 2:7) Other infor-

---

17. (a) What alleged inconsistency do some point to in the first two chapters of Genesis? (b) What is the basic reason for the supposed discrepancy?

18. How can we reconcile the apparent discrepancies between the two creation accounts in the early chapters of Genesis?

mation is then introduced as needed. We learn that after his creation Adam was to live in a garden in Eden. So the planting of the garden of Eden is now mentioned. (Genesis 2:8, 9, 15) Jehovah tells Adam to name "every wild beast of the field and every flying creature of the heavens." Now, then, is the time to mention that "Jehovah God was forming from the ground" all these creatures, although their creation began long before Adam appeared on the scene.—Genesis 2:19; 1:20, 24, 26.

Read the Account Carefully

19 Sometimes, all that is needed to resolve apparent contradictions is to read the account carefully and reason on the information provided. This is the case when we consider the conquest of Jerusalem by the Israelites. Jerusalem was listed as part of the inheritance of Benjamin, but we read that Benjamin's tribe was unable to conquer it. (Joshua 18:28; Judges 1:21) We also read that Judah was unable to conquer Jerusalem—as if it were part of that tribe's inheritance. Eventually, Judah defeated Jerusalem, burning it with fire. (Joshua 15:63; Judges 1:8) Hundreds of years later, however, David is also recorded as conquering Jerusalem. —2 Samuel 5:5-9.

20 At first glance, all of this might appear confusing, but there are in reality no contradictions. In fact, the boundary between Benjamin's inheritance and Judah's ran along the Valley of Hinnom, right

---

19. What apparent confusion exists in the Bible's account of the conquest of Jerusalem?

20, 21. By examining carefully all the relevant details, what emerges as the history of the Hebrew takeover of the city of Jerusalem?

through the ancient city of Jerusalem. What later came to be called the City of David actually lay in the territory of Benjamin, just as Joshua 18:28 says. But it is likely that the Jebusite city of Jerusalem spilled across the Valley of Hinnom and thus overlapped into Judah's territory, so that Judah, too, had to war against its Canaanite inhabitants.

21 Benjamin was unable to conquer the city. On one occasion, Judah did conquer Jerusalem and burn it. (Judges 1:8, 9) But Judah's forces evidently moved on, and some of the original inhabitants regained possession of the city. Later, they formed a pocket of resistance that neither Judah nor Benjamin could remove. Thus, the Jebusites continued in Jerusalem until David conquered the city hundreds of years later.

22 We meet up with a second example in the Gospels. Concerning Jesus' being led out to his death, in John's Gospel we read: "Bearing the torture stake for himself, he went out." (John 19:17) However, in Luke we read: "Now as they led him away, they laid hold of Simon, a certain native of Cyrene, coming from the country, and they placed the torture stake upon him to bear it behind Jesus." (Luke 23:26) Did Jesus carry the implement of his death, or did Simon carry it for him?

23 To begin with, Jesus evidently carried his own torture stake, as John points out. But later, as Matthew, Mark, and Luke testify, Simon of Cyrene was impressed into service to carry it for him the rest of the way to the place of execution.

22, 23. Who carried Jesus' torture stake to the place of execution?

Proof of Independence

24 True, there are some apparent inconsistencies in the Bible that are difficult to reconcile. But we should not assume that they are definite contradictions. Often it is merely a case of lack of complete information. The Bible provides enough knowledge to fill our spiritual need. But if it were to give us every detail about every event mentioned, it would be a huge, unwieldy library, rather than the handy, easy-to-carry volume that we have today.

25 Speaking of Jesus' ministry, the apostle John wrote with justifiable exaggeration: "There are, in fact, many other things also which Jesus did, which, if ever they were written in full detail, I suppose, the world itself could not contain the scrolls written." (John 21:25) It would be even more of an impossibility to record all the details of the long history of God's people from the patriarchs to the first-century Christian congregation!

26 Actually, the Bible is a miracle of condensation. It contains enough information to enable us to recognize it as more than merely a human work. Any variations it contains prove that the writers were truly independent witnesses. On the other hand, the outstanding unity of the Bible—which we will discuss in more detail in a future chapter—demonstrates without any doubt its divine origin. It is the word of God, not of man.

---

24. Why are we not surprised to find some apparent inconsistencies in the Bible, but what should we not conclude from this?

25. What does John say about the record of Jesus' ministry, and how does this help us to understand why the Bible does not give us every detail about every event?

26. The Bible contains enough information for us to be sure of what vital fact?

Science: Has It Proved the Bible Wrong?

In 1613 the Italian scientist Galileo published a work known as "Letters on Sunspots." In it, he presented evidence that the earth rotates around the sun, rather than the sun around the earth. By so doing, he set in motion a series of events that finally brought him before the Roman Catholic Inquisition under "vehement suspicion of heresy." Eventually, he was forced to "recant." Why was the idea that the earth moves around the sun viewed as heresy? Because Galileo's accusers claimed that it was contrary to what the Bible says.

IT IS widely held today that the Bible is unscientific, and some point to Galileo's experiences to prove it. But is this the case? When answering that question, we have to remember that the Bible is a book of prophecy, history, prayer, law, counsel, and knowledge about God. It does not claim to be a scientific textbook. Nevertheless, when the Bible does touch on scientific matters, what it says is completely accurate.

1. (Include introduction.) (a) What happened when Galileo suggested that the earth moved around the sun? (b) Although the Bible is not a science textbook, what do we find when we compare it with modern science?

Our Planet Earth

2 Consider, for example, what the Bible says about our planet, the earth. In the book of Job, we read: "[God] is stretching out the north over the empty place, hanging the earth upon nothing." (Job 26:7) Compare this with Isaiah's statement, when he says: "There is One who is dwelling above the circle of the earth." (Isaiah 40:22) The picture conveyed of a round earth 'hanging upon nothing' in "the empty place" reminds us strongly of the photographs taken by astronauts of the sphere of the earth floating in empty space.

3 Consider, too, the earth's amazing water cycle. Here is how *Compton's Encyclopedia* describes what happens: "Water . . . evaporates from the surface of the oceans into the atmosphere . . . Steadily moving air currents in the earth's atmosphere carry the moist air inland. When the air cools, the vapor condenses to form water droplets. These are seen most commonly as clouds. Often the droplets come together to form raindrops. If the atmosphere is cold enough, snowflakes form instead of raindrops. In either case, water that has traveled from an ocean

2. How does the Bible describe the earth's position in space?

3, 4. What is the earth's water cycle, and what does the Bible say about this?

The Bible's description of the earth hanging in space agrees very well with what astronauts have reported seeing

hundreds or even thousands of miles away falls to the earth's surface. There it gathers into streams or soaks into the ground and begins its journey back to the sea."[1]

4 This remarkable process, which makes life on dry land possible, was well described about 3,000 years ago in simple, straightforward terms in the Bible: "All streams run into the sea, yet the sea never overflows; back to the place from which the streams ran they return to run again."—Ecclesiastes 1:7, *The New English Bible*.

5 Perhaps even more remarkable is the Bible's insight into the history of mountains. Here is what a textbook on geology says: "From Pre-Cambrian times down to the present, the perpetual process of building and destroying mountains has continued. . . . Not only have mountains originated from the bottom of vanished seas, but they have often been submerged long after their formation, and then re-elevated."[2] Compare this with the poetic language of the psalmist: "With a watery deep just like a garment you covered [the earth]. The waters were standing above the very mountains. Mountains proceeded to ascend, valley plains proceeded to descend—to the place that you have founded for them."—Psalm 104:6, 8.

"In the Beginning"

6 The very first verse of the Bible states: "In the beginning God created the heavens and the earth." (Genesis 1:1) Observations have led scientists to the-

---

5. How is the psalmist's comment about the history of earth's mountains remarkably up-to-date?

6. What Bible statement is in harmony with current scientific theories about the origin of the universe?

orize that the material universe did indeed have a beginning. It has not existed for all time. Astronomer Robert Jastrow, an agnostic in religious matters, wrote: "The details differ, but the essential elements in the astronomical and biblical accounts of Genesis are the same: the chain of events leading to man commenced suddenly and sharply at a definite moment in time, in a flash of light and energy."[3]

7 True, many scientists, while believing that the universe had a beginning, do not accept the statement that *"God* created." Nevertheless, some now admit that it is difficult to ignore the evidence of some kind of intelligence behind everything. Physics professor Freeman Dyson comments: "The more I examine the universe and study the details of its architecture, the more evidence I find that the universe in some sense must have known that we were coming."

8 Dyson goes on to admit: "Being a scientist, trained in the habits of thought and language of the twentieth century rather than the eighteenth, I do not claim that the architecture of the universe proves the existence of God. I claim only that the architecture of the universe is consistent with the hypothesis that mind plays an essential role in its functioning."[4] His comment certainly betrays the skeptical attitude of our time. But putting that skepticism aside, one notes there is a remarkable harmony between modern science and the Bible's statement that "in the beginning God created the heavens and the earth."—Genesis 1:1.

7, 8. Although not admitting the role of God in the matter, what are many scientists forced to admit with regard to the origin of the universe?

Health and Sanitation

9 Consider the Bible's coverage of another field: health and sanitation. If an Israelite had a skin blemish suspected of being leprosy, he was put in isolation. "All the days that the plague is in him he will be unclean. He is unclean. He should dwell isolated. Outside the camp is his dwelling place." (Leviticus 13:46) Even infected garments were burned. (Leviticus 13:52) In those days, this was an effective way of preventing the spread of the infection.

10 Another important law had to do with the disposal of human excrement, which had to be buried outside the camp. (Deuteronomy 23:12, 13) This law no doubt saved Israel from many sicknesses. Even today, severe health problems are caused in some lands by the improper disposal of human wastes. If people in those lands would only follow the law written down thousands of years ago in the Bible, they would be much healthier.

11 The Bible's high standard of hygiene even involved mental health. A Bible proverb said: "A calm heart is the life of the fleshly organism, but jealousy

---

9. How does the Bible's law on infectious skin diseases reflect practical wisdom? (Job 12:9, 16a)

10. In what way would many in some lands benefit from following the Bible's counsel on hygiene?

11. What Bible counsel on mental health has been found to be practical?

The Bible does not get involved in saying whether the earth revolves around the sun or the sun revolves around the earth

is rottenness to the bones." (Proverbs 14:30) In recent years, medical research has demonstrated that our physical health is indeed affected by our mental attitude. For example, Doctor C. B. Thomas of Johns Hopkins University studied more than a thousand graduates over a period of 16 years, matching their psychological characteristics with their vulnerability to diseases. One thing she noted: The graduates most vulnerable to disease were those who were angrier and more anxious under stress.[5]

What Does the Bible Say?

12 If the Bible is so accurate in scientific fields, why did the Catholic Church say that Galileo's teaching that the earth moved around the sun was unscriptural? Because of the way the authorities interpreted certain Bible verses.[6] Were they correct? Let us read two of the passages they quoted and see.

13 One passage says: "The sun rises, the sun sets; then to its place it speeds and there it rises." (Ecclesiastes 1:5, *The Jerusalem Bible*) According to the Church's argument, expressions such as "the sun rises" and "the sun sets" mean that the sun, not the earth, is moving. But even today we say that the sun rises and sets, and most of us *know* that it is the earth that moves, not the sun. When we use expressions like these, we are merely describing the *apparent* motion of the sun as it appears to a human observer. The Bible writer was doing exactly the same.

14 The other passage says: "You fixed the earth

---

12. Why did the Catholic Church insist that Galileo's theory about the earth was heresy?

13, 14. What Bible verses did the Catholic Church misapply? Explain.

on its foundations, unshakeable for ever and ever." (Psalm 104:5, *The Jerusalem Bible*) This was interpreted to mean that after its creation the earth could never move. In fact, though, the verse stresses the permanence of the earth, not its immobility. The earth will never be 'shaken' out of existence, or destroyed, as other Bible verses confirm. (Psalm 37:29; Ecclesiastes 1:4) This scripture, too, has nothing to do with the relative motion of the earth and the sun. In Galileo's time, it was the Church, not the Bible, that hindered free scientific discussion.

Evolution and Creation

15 There is, however, an area where many would say that modern science and the Bible are hopelessly at odds. Most scientists believe the theory of evolution, which teaches that all living things evolved from a simple form of life that came into existence millions of years ago. The Bible, on the other hand, teaches that each major group of living things was specially created and reproduces only "according to its kind." Man, it says, was created "out of dust from the ground." (Genesis 1:21; 2:7) Is this a glaring scientific error in the Bible? Before deciding, let us look more closely at what science *knows,* as opposed to what it theorizes.

16 The theory of evolution was popularized during the last century by Charles Darwin. When he was on the Galápagos Islands in the Pacific, Darwin was

---

15. What is the theory of evolution, and how does it contradict the Bible?

16-18. (a) What was one observation that Charles Darwin made that led him to believe in evolution? (b) How can we argue that what Darwin observed in the Galápagos Islands does not contradict what the Bible says?

"Out of Dust"

"The World Book Encyclopedia" reports: "All the chemical elements that make up living things are also present in nonliving matter." In other words, the basic chemicals that go to make up living organisms, including man, are also found in the earth itself. This harmonizes with the Bible's statement: "And Jehovah God proceeded to form the man out of dust from the ground."—Genesis 2:7.

strongly impressed by the different species of finches on the different islands, which, he deduced, must all have descended from just one ancestral species. Partly because of this observation, he promoted the theory that all living things come from one original, simple form. The driving force behind the evolution of higher creatures from lower, he asserted, was natural selection, the survival of the fittest. Thanks to evolution, he claimed, land animals developed from fish, birds from reptiles, and so forth.

17 As a matter of fact, what Darwin *observed* in those isolated islands was not out of harmony with the Bible, which allows for variation within a major living kind. All the races of mankind, for example, came from just one original human pair. (Genesis 2:7, 22-24) So it is nothing strange that those different species of finches would spring from a common ancestral species. But they did remain finches. They did not evolve into hawks or eagles.

18 Neither the various species of finches nor anything else Darwin saw proved that all living things, whether they be sharks or sea gulls, elephants or

earthworms, have a common ancestor. Nevertheless, many scientists assert that evolution is no longer just a theory but that it is a fact. Others, while recognizing the theory's problems, say that they believe it anyway. It is popular to do so. We, however, need to know whether evolution has been proved to such an extent that the Bible must be wrong.

Is It Proved?

19 How can the theory of evolution be tested? The most obvious way is to examine the fossil record to see if a gradual change from one kind to another really happened. Did it? No, as a number of scientists honestly admit. One, Francis Hitching, writes: "When you look for links between major groups of animals, they simply aren't there."[7] So obvious is this lack of evidence in the fossil record that evolutionists have come up with alternatives to Darwin's theory of gradual change. The truth is, though, that the sudden appearance of animal kinds in the fossil record supports special creation much more than it does evolution.

20 Moreover, Hitching shows that living creatures are programmed to reproduce themselves exactly rather than evolve into something else. He says: "Living cells duplicate themselves with near-total fidelity. The degree of error is so tiny that no man-made machine can approach it. There are also built-in constraints. Plants reach a certain size and refuse to grow any larger. Fruit flies refuse to be-

---

19. Does the fossil record support evolution or creation?
20. Why does the way living cells reproduce not allow for evolution to take place?

'In God's Image'

Some point to physical similarities between man and some of the animals to prove their relationship. They have to agree, though, that man's mental capacities are far superior to those of any animal. Why does man have the ability to make plans and organize the world around him, the capacity for love, a high intelligence, a conscience, and a concept of past, present, and future? Evolution cannot answer this. But the Bible does, when it says: "God proceeded to create the man in his image, in God's image he created him." (Genesis 1:27) As far as man's mental and moral abilities and potential are concerned, he is a reflection of his heavenly Father.

come anything but fruit flies under any circumstances yet devised."[8] Mutations induced by scientists in fruit flies over many decades failed to force these to evolve into something else.

The Origin of Life

21 Another thorny question that evolutionists have failed to answer is: What was the origin of life? How did the first simple form of life—from which we are all supposed to have descended—come into existence? Centuries ago, this would not have appeared to be a problem. Most people then thought that flies could develop from decaying meat and that a pile of old rags could spontaneously produce mice. But, more than a hundred years ago, the French chemist Louis Pasteur clearly demonstrated that life can come only from preexisting life.

---

21. What conclusion proved by Louis Pasteur poses a grave problem for evolutionists?

22 So how do evolutionists explain the source of life? According to the most popular theory, a chance combination of chemicals and energy sparked a spontaneous generation of life millions of years ago. What about the principle that Pasteur proved? *The World Book Encyclopedia* explains: "Pasteur showed that life cannot arise spontaneously under the chemical and physical conditions present on the earth today. Billions of years ago, however, the chemical and physical conditions on the earth were far different"![9]

23 Even under far different conditions, though, there is a huge gap between nonliving matter and the simplest living thing. Michael Denton, in his book *Evolution: A Theory in Crisis,* says: "Between a living cell and the most highly ordered non-biological system, such as a crystal or a snowflake, there is a chasm as vast and absolute as it is possible to conceive."[10] The idea that nonliving material could come to life by some haphazard chance is so remote as to be impossible. The Bible's explanation, that 'life came from life' in that life was created by God, is convincingly in harmony with the facts.

Why Not Creation

24 Despite the problems inherent in the theory of evolution, belief in creation is viewed today as unscientific, even eccentric. Why is this? Why does even an authority such as Fran-

The Bible presents an accurate description of the earth's water cycle

---

22, 23. According to evolutionists, how did life get started, but what do the facts show?

24. In spite of the theory's problems, why do most scientists still cling to the theory of evolution?

cis Hitching, who honestly points up the weaknesses of evolution, reject the idea of creation?[11] Michael Denton explains that evolution, with all its failings, will continue to be taught because theories related to creation "invoke frankly supernatural causes."[12] In other words, the fact that creation involves a Creator makes it unacceptable. Surely, this is the same kind of circular reasoning that we met up with in the case of miracles: Miracles are impossible because they are miraculous!

25 Besides, the theory of evolution itself is deeply suspect from a scientific viewpoint. Michael Denton goes on to say: "Being basically a theory of historical reconstruction, [Darwin's theory of evolution] is impossible to verify by experiment or direct observation as is normal in science. . . . Moreover, the theory of evolution deals with a series of unique events, the origin of life, the origin of intelligence and so on. Unique events are unrepeatable and cannot be subjected to any sort of experimental investigation."[13] The truth is that the theory of evolution, despite its popularity, is full of gaps and problems. It gives no good reason to reject the Bible's account of the

25. What weakness of evolution, scientifically speaking, shows that it is not a valid alternative to creation in explaining the origin of life?

origin of life. The first chapter of Genesis provides a completely reasonable account of how these "unrepeatable" "unique events" came about during creative 'days' that stretched through millenniums of time.*

What About the Flood?

26 Many point to another supposed contradiction between the Bible and modern science. In the book of Genesis, we read that thousands of years ago the wickedness of men was so great that God determined to destroy them. However, he instructed the righteous man Noah to build a large wooden vessel, an ark. Then God brought a flood upon mankind. Only Noah and his family survived, together with representatives of all the animal species. The Flood was so great that "all the tall mountains that were under the whole heavens came to be covered."—Genesis 7:19.

27 Where did all the water come from to cover the whole earth? The Bible itself answers. Early in the creation process, when the expanse of the atmosphere began to take shape, there came to be "waters . . . beneath the expanse" and "waters . . . above the expanse." (Genesis 1:7; 2 Peter 3:5) When the Flood came, the Bible says: "The floodgates of the heavens

---

* A much more detailed discussion of the subject of evolution and creation is found in the book *Life—How Did It Get Here? By Evolution or by Creation?* published in 1985 by the Watchtower Bible and Tract Society of New York, Inc.

26, 27. (a) What does the Bible say about the Flood? (b) From where, in part, must the floodwaters have come?

were opened." (Genesis 7:11) Evidently, the "waters . . . above the expanse" fell and provided much of the water for the inundation.

28 Modern textbooks are inclined to discount a universal flood. So we have to ask: Is the Flood just a myth, or did it really happen? Before answering that, we should note that later worshipers of Jehovah accepted the Flood as genuine history; they did not regard it as a myth. Isaiah, Jesus, Paul, and Peter were among those who referred to it as something that really happened. (Isaiah 54:9; Matthew 24:37-39; Hebrews 11:7; 1 Peter 3:20, 21; 2 Peter 2:5; 3:5-7) But there are questions that have to be answered about this universal Deluge.

The Floodwaters

29 First, is not the idea of the whole earth's being flooded too farfetched? Not really. Indeed, to some extent the earth is still flooded. Seventy percent of it is covered by water and only 30 percent is dry land. Moreover, 75 percent of the earth's fresh water is locked up in glaciers and polar ice caps. If all this ice were to melt, the sea level would rise much higher. Cities like New York and Tokyo would disappear.

30 Further, *The New Encyclopædia Britannica* says: "The average depth of all the seas has been estimated at 3,790 metres (12,430 feet), a figure considerably larger than that of the average elevation of the land above the sea level, which is 840 metres

---

28. How did ancient servants of God, including Jesus, view the Flood?

29, 30. What facts about the earth's water supply show that the Flood is feasible?

(2,760 feet). If the average depth is multiplied by its respective surface area, the volume of the World Ocean is 11 times the volume of the land above sea level."[14] So, if everything were leveled out—if the mountains were flattened and the deep sea basins filled in—the sea would cover the whole earth to a depth of thousands of meters.

31 For the Flood to have happened, the pre-Flood sea basins would have to have been shallower, and the mountains lower than they are now. Is this possible? Well, one textbook says: "Where the mountains of the world now tower to dizzy heights, oceans and plains once, millions of years ago, stretched out in flat monotony. . . . The movements of the continental plates cause the land both to rear up to heights where only the hardiest of animals and plants can survive and, at the other extreme, to plunge and lie in hidden splendor deep beneath the surface of the sea."[15] Since the mountains and sea basins rise and fall, it is apparent that at one time the mountains were not as high as they are now and the great sea basins were not as deep.

32 What happened to the floodwaters after the Flood? They must have drained into the sea basins. How? Scientists believe that the continents rest on huge plates. Movement of

If the earth were leveled, with no mountains or abysses, it would be completely covered with a deep layer of water

31. (a) For the Flood to have happened, what must have been the situation with the pre-Flood earth? (b) What shows it is feasible that the mountains were lower and that the sea basins were shallower before the Flood?

32. What must have happened to the waters of the Flood? Explain.

these plates can cause changes in the level of the earth's surface. In some places today, there are great underwater abysses more than six miles deep at the plate boundaries.[16] It is quite likely that —perhaps triggered by the Flood itself—the plates moved, the sea bottom sank, and the great trenches opened, allowing the water to drain off the land.*

Traces of the Flood?

33 If we grant that a great flood *could* have happened, why have scientists found no trace of it? Perhaps they have, but they interpret the evidence some other way. For example, orthodox science teaches that the surface of the earth has been shaped in many places by powerful glaciers during a series of ice ages. But apparent evidence of glacial activity can sometimes be the result of water action. Very

* The book *Planet Earth—Glacier* draws attention to the way water in the form of ice sheets depresses the surface of the earth. For example, it says: "If the Greenland ice were to disappear, the island would eventually rebound some 2,000 feet." In view of this, the effect of a sudden global flood on parts of the earth's crust could well have been catastrophic.[17]

33, 34. (a) What evidence do scientists already possess that may be evidence for the Flood? (b) Is it reasonable to say that scientists may be misreading the evidence?

Mammoths were found that were quick-frozen after their death

likely, then, some of the evidence for the Flood is being misread as evidence of an ice age.

34 Similar mistakes have been made. Concerning the time when scientists were developing their theory of ice ages, we read: "They were finding ice ages at every stage of the geologic history, in keeping with the philosophy of uniformity. Careful reexamination of the evidence in recent years, however, has rejected many of these ice ages; formations once identified as glacial moraines have been reinterpreted as beds laid down by mudflows, submarine landslides and turbidity currents: avalanches of turbid water that carry silt, sand and gravel out over the deep-ocean floor."[18]

35 Another evidence for the Flood appears to exist in the fossil record. At one time, according to this record, great saber-toothed tigers stalked their prey in Europe, horses larger than any now living roamed North America, and mammoths foraged in Siberia. Then, all around the world, species of mammals became extinct. At the same time, there was a sudden change of climate. Tens of thousands of mammoths were killed and quick-frozen in Siberia.* Alfred Wal-

---

* One estimate says five million.

35, 36. What evidence in the fossil record and in geology may be related to the Flood? Explain.

lace, the well-known contemporary of Charles Darwin, considered that such a widespread destruction must have been caused by some exceptional worldwide event.[19] Many have argued that this event was the Flood.

36 An editorial in the magazine *Biblical Archaeologist* observed: "It is important to remember that the story of a great flood is one of the most widespread traditions in human culture . . . Nevertheless behind the oldest traditions found in Near Eastern sources, there may well be an actual flood of gigantic proportions dating from one of the pluvial periods . . . many thousands of years ago."[20] The pluvial periods were times when the surface of the earth was much wetter than now. Freshwater lakes around the world were much larger. It is theorized that the wetness was caused by heavy rains associated with the end of the ice ages. But some have suggested that on one occasion the extreme wetness of the earth's surface was a result of the Flood.

Mankind Did Not Forget

37 Geology professor John McCampbell once

37, 38. How does one scientist show that, according to the evidence, the Flood *might* have happened, and how do we know that it did?

Louis Pasteur proved that life can come only from already-existing life

wrote: "The essential differences between Biblical catastrophism [the Flood] and evolutionary uniformitarianism are not over the factual data of geology but over the interpretations of those data. The interpretation preferred will depend largely upon the background and presuppositions of the individual student."[21]

38 That the Flood *did* happen is seen in the fact that mankind never forgot it. All around the world, in locations as far apart as Alaska and the South Sea Islands, there are ancient stories about it. Native, pre-Columbian civilizations of America, as well as Aborigines of Australia, all have stories about the Flood. While some of the accounts differ in detail, the basic fact that the earth was flooded and only a few humans were saved in a man-made vessel comes through in nearly all versions. The only explanation for such a widespread acceptance is that the Flood was a historical event.*

39 Thus, in essential features the Bible is in harmony with modern science. Where there is a conflict between the two, the scientists' evidence is questionable. Where they agree, the Bible is often so accurate that we have to believe it got its information from a superhuman intelligence. Indeed, the Bible's agreement with proved science provides further evidence that it is God's word, not man's.

---

* For more information on the Flood, see *Insight on the Scriptures,* published by the Watchtower Bible and Tract Society of New York, Inc., Volume 1, pages 327, 328, 609-612.

---

39. What additional proof have we seen of the fact that the Bible is God's word, not man's?

Prophecies That Came True

Humans cannot foretell the future with any certainty. Time and again their efforts at prediction fail miserably. So a book of prophecies that did come true has to attract our attention. The Bible is such a book.

MANY Bible prophecies have come true in such detail that critics claim they were written after the fulfillment. But such claims are untrue. God, being almighty, is fully capable of prophesying. (Isaiah 41:21-26; 42:8, 9; 46:8-10) Biblical prophecies that came true are evidence of divine inspiration, not of late authorship. We will look now at some outstanding prophecies that came true—providing additional proof that the Bible is God's word, not just man's.

The Exile in Babylon

[2] Hezekiah was king in Jerusalem for about 30 years. In 740 B.C.E. he witnessed the destruction of his northern neighbor Israel at the hands of Assyria. In 732 B.C.E. he experienced God's saving power,

---

1. (Include introduction.) What is proved by the fact that the Bible records prophecies that came true?

2, 3. What led up to King Hezekiah's showing all the treasures of his house and dominion to envoys from Babylon?

when the Assyrian attempt to conquer Jerusalem had failed, with catastrophic results to the invader. —Isaiah 37:33-38.

3 Now, Hezekiah is receiving a delegation from Merodach-baladan, king of Babylon. On the surface, the ambassadors are there to congratulate Hezekiah on his recovery from a severe illness. Likely, though, Merodach-baladan sees Hezekiah as a possible ally against the world power of Assyria. Hezekiah does nothing to dispel such an idea when he shows the visiting Babylonians all the wealth of his house and dominion. Perhaps he, too, wants allies against a possible return of the Assyrians.—Isaiah 39:1, 2.

4 Isaiah is the outstanding prophet of that time, and he quickly discerns Hezekiah's indiscretion. He knows that Hezekiah's surest defense is Jehovah, not Babylon, and tells him that his act of showing

---

4. What tragic consequence of Hezekiah's mistake did Isaiah prophesy?

Archaeologists have discovered that the destruction of Jerusalem by Nebuchadnezzar was a total one

the Babylonians his wealth will lead to tragedy. "Days are coming," says Isaiah, "and all that is in your own house and that your forefathers have stored up down to this day will actually be carried to Babylon." Jehovah decreed: "Nothing will be left." —Isaiah 39:5, 6.

5 Back in the eighth century B.C.E., it may have seemed unlikely for that prophecy to be fulfilled. One hundred years later, however, the situation changed. Babylon replaced Assyria as the dominant world power, while Judah became so degraded, religiously speaking, that God withdrew his blessing. Now, another prophet, Jeremiah, was inspired to repeat Isaiah's warning. Jeremiah proclaimed: "I will bring [the Babylonians] against this land and against its inhabitants . . . And all this land must become a devastated place, an object of astonishment, and these nations will have to serve the king of Babylon seventy years."—Jeremiah 25:9, 11.

6 About four years after Jeremiah uttered that prophecy, the Babylonians made Judah part of their empire. Three years after that, they took some Jewish captives, along with some of the wealth of the temple at Jerusalem, to Babylon. Eight years later, Judah revolted and was again invaded by the Babylonian king, Nebuchadnezzar. This time, the city and its temple were destroyed. All its wealth, and the Jews themselves, were carried off to distant Babylon, just as Isaiah and Jeremiah had foretold. —2 Chronicles 36:6, 7, 12, 13, 17-21.

5, 6. (a) What did Jeremiah say in confirmation of Isaiah's prophecy? (b) In what way were the prophecies of Isaiah and Jeremiah fulfilled?

[7] *The Archaeological Encyclopedia of the Holy Land* notes that when the Babylonian onslaught was over, "the destruction of the city [Jerusalem] was a total one."[1] Archaeologist W. F. Albright states: "Excavation and surface exploration in Judah have proved that the towns of Judah were not only completely destroyed by the Chaldeans in their two invasions, but were not reoccupied for generations—often never again in history."[2] Thus, archaeology confirms the shocking fulfillment of this prophecy.

The Fate of Tyre

[8] Ezekiel was another ancient writer who recorded divinely inspired prophecies. He prophesied from the end of the seventh century B.C.E. on into the sixth—that is, during the years leading up to the destruction of Jerusalem and then during the first decades of the Jews' exile in Babylon. Even some modern critics agree that the book was written at approximately this time.

[9] Ezekiel recorded a striking prophecy about the destruction of Israel's northern neighbor Tyre, which had gone from a position of friendship with God's people to one of enmity. (1 Kings 5:1-9; Psalm 83:2-8) He wrote: "This is what the Sovereign Lord Jehovah has said, 'Here I am against you, O Tyre, and I will bring up against you many nations, just as the sea brings up its waves. And they will certainly bring the walls of Tyre to ruin and tear down her towers, and I will scrape her dust away from her and make her a shining, bare surface of a crag. . . . And

---

7. How does archaeology testify to the fulfillment of the prophecies of Isaiah and Jeremiah concerning Jerusalem?
8, 9. What prophecy did Ezekiel utter against Tyre?

Photograph of modern Tyre. Hardly a vestige remains of the Tyre the prophets of Israel knew

your stones and your woodwork and your dust they will place in the very midst of the water.'"—Ezekiel 26:3, 4, 12.

10 Did this really happen? Well, a few years after Ezekiel uttered the prophecy, the king of Babylon, Nebuchadnezzar, laid siege to Tyre. (Ezekiel 29: 17, 18) It was not, however, an easy siege. Tyre was partially situated on the mainland (the part called Old Tyre). But part of the city was on an island about half a mile offshore. Nebuchadnezzar besieged the island for 13 years before it finally submitted to him.

11 It was, however, in 332 B.C.E. that Ezekiel's prophecy was finally fulfilled in all its details. At that time, Alexander the Great, the conqueror from Macedonia, was invading Asia. Tyre, secure on its island location, held out against him. Alexander did not want to leave a potential enemy at his rear, but he did not want to spend years in a siege of Tyre, as Nebuchadnezzar had done.

12 How did he solve this military problem? He built a land bridge, or mole, across to the island, so

10-12. When was Ezekiel's prophecy finally fulfilled, and how?

that his soldiers could march across and attack the island city. Notice, though, what he used to build the mole. *The Encyclopedia Americana* reports: "With the debris of the mainland portion of the city, which he had demolished, he built a huge mole in 332 to join the island to the mainland." After a relatively short siege, the island city was destroyed. Moreover, Ezekiel's prophecy was fulfilled in all its details. Even the 'stones and woodwork and dust' of Old Tyre were 'placed in the very midst of the water.'

13 A 19th-century traveler commented on what was left of ancient Tyre in his day, saying: "Of the original Tyre known to Solomon and the prophets of Israel, not a vestige remains except in its rock-cut sepulchres on the mountain sides, and in foundation walls . . . Even the island, which Alexander the Great, in his siege of the city, converted into a cape by filling up the water between it and the mainland, contains no distinguishable relics of an earlier period than that of the Crusades. The modern town, all of which is comparatively new, occupies the northern half of what was once the island, while nearly all the remainder of the surface is covered with undistinguishable ruins."[3]

Babylon's Turn

14 Back in the eighth century B.C.E., Isaiah, the prophet who warned the Jews of their coming subjugation by Babylon, also foretold something astounding: the total annihilation of Babylon itself. He fore-

---

13. How did a 19th-century traveler describe the site of ancient Tyre?

14, 15. What prophecies did Isaiah and Jeremiah record against Babylon?

told this in graphic detail: "Here I am arousing against them the Medes . . . And Babylon, the decoration of kingdoms, the beauty of the pride of the Chaldeans, must become as when God overthrew Sodom and Gomorrah. She will never be inhabited, nor will she reside for generation after generation." —Isaiah 13:17-20.

15 The prophet Jeremiah also foretold the fall of Babylon, which would take place many years later. And he included an interesting detail: "There is a devastation upon her waters, and they must be dried up. . . . The mighty men of Babylon have ceased to fight. They have kept sitting in the strong places. Their mightiness has run dry."—Jeremiah 50:38; 51:30.

16 In 539 B.C.E., the time of Babylon's rule as the preeminent world power came to an end when the vigorous Persian ruler Cyrus, accompanied by the army of Media, marched against the city. What

---

16. When was Babylon conquered, and by whom?

Tourists who visit the site of ancient Babylon are witnesses of the fulfillment of the prophecies against the city

Cyrus found, however, was formidable. Babylon was surrounded by huge walls and seemed impregnable. The great river Euphrates, too, ran through the city and made an important contribution to its defenses.

17 The Greek historian Herodotus describes how Cyrus handled the problem: "He placed a portion of his army at the point where the river enters the city, and another body at the back of the place where it issues forth, with orders to march into the town by the bed of the stream, as soon as the water became shallow enough . . . He turned the Euphrates by a canal into the basin [an artificial lake dug by a previous ruler of Babylon], which was then a marsh, on which the river sank to such an extent that the natural bed of the stream became fordable. Hereupon the Persians who had been left for the purpose at Babylon by the river-side, entered the stream, which had now sunk so as to reach about midway up a man's thigh, and thus got into the town."[4]

18 In this way the city fell, as Jeremiah and Isaiah had warned. But notice the detailed fulfillment of prophecy. There was literally 'a devastation upon her waters, and they were dried up.' It was the lowering of the waters of the Euphrates that enabled Cyrus to gain access to the city. Did 'the mighty men of Babylon cease to fight,' as Jeremiah had warned? The Bible—as well as the Greek historians Herodotus and Xenophon—records that the Babylonians were actually feasting when the Persian as-

---

17, 18. (a) In what way was there "a devastation upon [Babylon's] waters"? (b) Why did Babylon's 'mighty men cease to fight'?

sault occurred.[5] The Nabonidus Chronicle, an official cuneiform inscription, says that Cyrus' troops entered Babylon "without battle," likely meaning without a major pitched battle.[6] Evidently, Babylon's mighty men did not do much to protect her.

19 What about the forecast that Babylon would "never be inhabited" again? That was not fulfilled immediately in 539 B.C.E. But unerringly the prophecy came true. After her fall, Babylon was the center of a number of rebellions, until 478 B.C.E. when she was destroyed by Xerxes. At the end of the fourth century, Alexander the Great planned to restore her, but he died before the work had progressed very far. From then on, the city just declined. There were still people living there in the first century of our Common Era, but today all that is left of ancient Babylon is a heap of ruins in Iraq. Even if her ruins should be partially restored, Babylon would be just a tourist showpiece, not a living, vibrant city. Her desolate site bears witness to the final fulfillment of the inspired prophecies against her.

The March of World Powers

20 In the sixth century B.C.E., during the Jewish exile in Babylon, another prophet, Daniel, was inspired to record some remarkable visions foretelling the future course of world events. In one, Daniel describes a number of symbolic animals that

---

19. Was the prophecy that Babylon would "never be inhabited" fulfilled? Explain.

20, 21. What prophecy did Daniel see of the march of world powers, and how was this fulfilled?

displace one another on the world scene. An angel explains that these animals foreshadow the march of world powers from that time onward. Speaking of the final two beasts, he says: "The ram that you saw possessing the two horns stands for the kings of Media and Persia. And the hairy he-goat stands for the king of Greece; and as for the great horn that was between its eyes, it stands for the first king. And that one having been broken, so that there were four that finally stood up instead of it, there are four kingdoms from his nation that will stand up, but not with his power."—Daniel 8:20-22.

21 This prophetic foreview was fulfilled exactly. The Babylonian Empire was overthrown by Medo-Persia, which, 200 years later, gave way to the Greek

Daniel's prophecies of the march of world powers were fulfilled so accurately that modern critics think they were written after the fulfillment

world power. The Greek Empire was spearheaded by Alexander the Great, "the great horn." However, after Alexander's death, his generals fought among themselves for power, and eventually the far-flung empire broke into four smaller empires, "four kingdoms."

22 In Daniel chapter 7, a somewhat similar vision also looked far into the future. The Babylonian world power was pictured by a lion, the Persian by a bear, and the Greek by a leopard with four wings on its back and four heads. Then, Daniel sees another wild beast, "fearsome and terrible and unusually strong . . . , and it had ten horns." (Daniel 7: 2-7) This fourth wild beast prefigured the powerful Roman Empire, which began to develop about three centuries after Daniel recorded this prophecy.

23 The angel prophesied regarding Rome: "As for the fourth beast, there is a fourth kingdom that will come to be on the earth, that will be different from all the other kingdoms; and it will devour all the earth and will trample it down and crush it." (Daniel 7:23) H. G. Wells, in his book *A Pocket History of the World,* says: "This new Roman power which arose to dominate the western world in the second and first

---

22. In a related prophecy of the march of world powers, what additional world power was prophesied?
23. In what way was the fourth wild beast of Daniel's prophecy "different from all the other kingdoms"?

centuries B.C. was in several respects a different thing from any of the great empires that had hitherto prevailed in the civilised world."[7] It started as a republic and continued as a monarchy. Unlike previous empires, it was not the creation of any one conqueror but grew relentlessly over the centuries. It lasted much, much longer and controlled far more territory than any previous empire.

24 What, though, about the ten horns of this huge beast? The angel said: "And as for the ten horns, out of that kingdom there are ten kings that will rise up; and still another one will rise up after them, and he himself will be different from the first ones, and three kings he will humiliate." (Daniel 7:24) How did this work out?

25 Well, when the Roman Empire started to deteriorate in the fifth century C.E., it was not immediately replaced by another world power. Rather, it disintegrated into a number of kingdoms, "ten kings." Finally, the British Empire defeated the three rival empires of Spain, France, and the Netherlands to become the major world power. Thus did the newcomer 'horn' humiliate "three kings."

Daniel's Prophecies—After the Fact?

26 The Bible indicates that the book of Daniel was written during the sixth century B.C.E. However, the fulfillments of its prophecies are so exact that critics claim it must have been written about

---

24, 25. (a) How did the ten horns of the wild beast make their appearance? (b) What struggle between the horns of the wild beast did Daniel foresee?

26. When do critics claim that Daniel was written, and why?

165 B.C.E., when a number of the prophecies had already been fulfilled.[8] Despite the fact that the only *real* reason for making this claim is that Daniel's prophecies were fulfilled, this late date for the writing of Daniel is presented as an established fact in many reference works.

27 Against such a theory, though, we must weigh the following facts. First, the book was alluded to in Jewish works produced during the second century B.C.E., such as the first book of Maccabees. Also, it was included in the Greek *Septuagint* version, the translation of which began in the third century B.C.E.[9] Third, fragments of copies of Daniel were among the more frequently found works in the Dead Sea Scrolls—and these fragments are believed to date to about 100 B.C.E.[10] Clearly, soon after Daniel was supposedly written, it was already widely known and respected: strong evidence that it was produced long before critics say it was.

28 Further, Daniel contains historical details that would have been unknown to a second-century writer. Outstanding is the case of Belshazzar, the ruler of Babylon who was killed when Babylon fell in 539 B.C.E. The major non-Biblical sources of our knowledge of the fall of Babylon are Herodotus (fifth century), Xenophon (fifth and fourth centuries), and Berossus (third century). None of these knew about Belshazzar.[11] How unlikely that a second-century writer would have had information that had been unavailable to these earlier authors! The record concerning Belshazzar in Daniel

---

27, 28. What are some of the facts that prove that Daniel was not written in 165 B.C.E.?

chapter 5 is a strong argument that Daniel wrote his book before these other writers wrote theirs.*

29 Finally, there are a number of prophecies in Daniel that were fulfilled long after 165 B.C.E. One of these was the prophecy about the Roman Empire, mentioned earlier. Another is a remarkable prophecy foretelling the arrival of Jesus, the Messiah.

The Coming of the Anointed One

30 This prophecy is recorded in Daniel, chapter 9, and reads as follows: "Seventy weeks [of years, or four hundred and ninety years] are decreed upon your people and upon your holy city."# (Daniel 9:24, *The Amplified Bible*) What was to happen during these 490 years? We read: "From the going forth of the commandment to restore and to build Jerusalem

* See Chapter 4, "How Believable Is the 'Old Testament'?" paragraphs 16 and 17.

In this translation, the words in brackets have been added by the translator to clarify the meaning.

29. Why is it impossible that the book of Daniel was written after the fulfillment of the prophecies therein?

30, 31. (a) What prophecy of Daniel predicted the time of Messiah's appearance? (b) How can we calculate, based on Daniel's prophecy, the year when Messiah was due to appear?

Daniel prophesied the exact time when the Messiah would appear in Israel

until [the coming of] the anointed one, a prince, shall be seven weeks [of years], and sixty-two weeks [of years]." (Daniel 9:25, *AB*) So this is a prophecy about the time of the coming of "the anointed one," the Messiah. How was it fulfilled?

31 The command to restore and to build Jerusalem 'went forth' in "the twentieth year of Artaxerxes the king" of Persia, that is, in 455 B.C.E. (Nehemiah 2:1-9) By the end of 49 years (7 weeks of years), much of Jerusalem's glory had been restored. And then, counting the full 483 years (7 plus 62 weeks of years) from 455 B.C.E., we arrive at 29 C.E. This was, in fact, "the fifteenth year of the reign of Tiberius Caesar," the year when Jesus was baptized by John the Baptizer. (Luke 3:1) At that time, Jesus was publicly identified as God's Son and began his ministry of preaching the good news to the Jewish nation. (Matthew 3:13-17; 4:23) He became the "anointed one," or Messiah.

32 The prophecy adds: "And after the sixty-two weeks [of years] shall the anointed one be cut off." It also says: "And he shall enter into a strong and firm covenant with the many for one week [seven years]; and in the midst of the week he shall cause the sacrifice and offering to cease." (Daniel 9:26, 27, *AB*) In harmony with this, Jesus went exclusively to "the many," the fleshly Jews. On occasion, he also preached to the Samaritans, who believed some of the Scriptures but had formed a sect separate from mainstream Judaism. Then, "in the midst of the week," after three and a half years of preaching, he

---

32. According to Daniel's prophecy, how long would Jesus' earthly ministry be, and what would happen at the end of it?

gave up his life as a sacrifice and was thus "cut off." This spelled the end of the Mosaic Law with its sacrifices and gift offerings. (Galatians 3:13, 24, 25) Hence, by his death, Jesus caused "the sacrifice and offering to cease."

33 Nevertheless, for another three and a half years the newborn Christian congregation witnessed solely to Jews and, later, to the related Samaritans. In 36 C.E., however, at the end of the 70 weeks of years, the apostle Peter was guided to preach to a Gentile, Cornelius. (Acts 10:1-48) Now, the "covenant with the many" was no longer limited to the Jews. Salvation was preached also to the uncircumcised Gentiles.

34 Because the Jewish nation rejected Jesus and conspired to have him executed, Jehovah did not protect them when the Romans came and destroyed Jerusalem in 70 C.E. Thus, Daniel's further words were fulfilled: "And the people of the other prince who shall come will destroy the city and the sanctuary. Its end shall come with a flood, and even to the end there shall be war." (Daniel 9:26b, *AB*) This second "prince" was Titus, the Roman general who destroyed Jerusalem in 70 C.E.

Prophecy That Was Inspired

35 In this way, Daniel's prophecy of the 70 weeks was fulfilled in a remarkably exact manner. Indeed, many of the prophecies recorded in the Hebrew

---

33. For how long would Jehovah deal exclusively with the Jews, and what event marked the end of this period?
34. In harmony with Daniel's prophecy, what happened to fleshly Israel because they rejected the Messiah?
35. What additional prophecies about Jesus came true?

Scriptures were fulfilled during the first century, and a number of these had to do with Jesus. The place of Jesus' birth, his zeal for God's house, his preaching activity, his betrayal for 30 pieces of silver, the manner of his death, the fact that lots were cast for his garments—all these details were prophesied in the Hebrew Scriptures. Their fulfillment proved without a doubt that Jesus was the Messiah, and it demonstrated again that the prophecies were inspired.—Micah 5:2; Luke 2:1-7; Zechariah 11:12; 12:10; Matthew 26:15; 27:35; Psalm 22:18; 34:20; John 19:33-37.

All prophecies that were due to be fulfilled came true. Things happened exactly the way the Bible said they would

[36] In fact, all the Bible's prophecies that were due to be fulfilled have come true. Things have happened exactly in the way the Bible said they would. This is strong evidence that the Bible is God's Word. There must have been more than human wisdom behind those prophetic utterances for them to have been so accurate.

[37] But there are other predictions in the Bible that were not fulfilled in those times. Why? Because they were due to be fulfilled in our own day, and even in our future. The reliability of those ancient prophecies makes us confident that these other predictions will without fail come true. As we will see in the next chapter, this is indeed the case.

36, 37. What do we learn from the fact that Biblical prophecies have come true, and what confidence does this knowledge give us?

Chapter 10

A Bible Prophecy You Have Seen Fulfilled

Have you ever wondered why things are so different today compared with the way they were a hundred years ago? Some things are better. In many lands, diseases that killed in the past are now routinely cured, and the average person enjoys a standard of living undreamed of by his ancestors. On the other hand, our century has seen the worst wars and some of the worst atrocities in all history. Mankind's prosperity—even his continued existence—is threatened by a population explosion, a pollution problem, and a vast, international stockpile of nuclear, biological, and chemical weapons. Why is the 20th century so different from previous centuries?

THE answer to this question has to do with a remarkable Bible prophecy that you have seen fulfilled. It is a prophecy that Jesus himself uttered and that, besides giving proof of the inspiration of the Bible, indicates that we are living close to very

---

1. (Include introduction.) (a) How has the 20th century differed from previous centuries? (b) What will help us to understand why our times are so different?

dramatic changes in the world scene. What is this prophecy? And how do we know that it is being fulfilled?

Jesus' Great Prophecy

2 The Bible tells us that shortly before Jesus' death, his disciples were discussing the great temple buildings in Jerusalem; they were impressed by their size and apparent durability. But Jesus said: "Do you not behold all these things? Truly I say to you, By no means will a stone be left here upon a stone and not be thrown down."—Matthew 24:1, 2.

3 Jesus' disciples must have been surprised at his words and later came to him for more information, saying: "Tell us, When will these things be, and what will be the sign of your presence and of the conclusion of the system of things?" (Matthew 24:3) Jesus' answer is found in the remainder of Matthew chapters 24 and 25. His words are recorded, too, in Mark chapter 13 and Luke chapter 21. This was clearly the most important prophecy uttered by Jesus while he was on earth.

4 In fact, Jesus' disciples were asking about more than one thing. First, they raised the question: "When will these things be?" that is, When will Jerusalem and its temple be destroyed? Further, they wanted to know the sign that would indicate that Jesus' presence as King of God's heavenly Kingdom had begun and that the end of this system of things was at hand.

2, 3. What question did Jesus' disciples ask him, and where do we find his answer?

4. About what different things were Jesus' disciples asking?

5 In his answer, Jesus took both points into consideration. Many of his words were actually fulfilled back in the first century, during the years that led up to the terrible destruction of Jerusalem in 70 C.E. (Matthew 24:4-22) But his prophecy was to have an even greater significance later, in our own days, in fact. What, then, did Jesus say? He began by uttering the words recorded in verses 7 and 8: "Nation will rise against nation and kingdom against kingdom, and there will be food shortages and earthquakes in one place after another. All these things are a beginning of pangs of distress."

6 Clearly, Jesus' presence as heavenly King would be marked by great turmoil on earth. This is confirmed by a parallel prophecy found in the book of Revelation: the vision of the four horsemen of the Apocalypse. (Revelation 6:1-8) The first of these horsemen pictures Jesus himself as conquering King. The other riders with their steeds picture happenings on earth that mark the beginning of Jesus' reign: war, famine, and untimely death through various agents. Do we see these two prophecies fulfilled today?

War!

7 Let us look at them more closely. First, Jesus said: "Nation will rise against nation and kingdom against kingdom." This was a prophecy of war. The

---

5. (a) What initial fulfillment was there of Jesus' prophecy, but when would his words have their complete fulfillment? (b) How did Jesus begin his answer to the disciples' question?

6. Jesus' words in Matthew 24:7, 8 remind us of what parallel prophecy?

7. What is prophetically prefigured by the ride of the second horseman of the Apocalypse?

second of the four horsemen of the Apocalypse similarly prefigured war. We read: “Another came forth, a fiery-colored horse; and to the one seated upon it there was granted to take peace away from the earth so that they should slaughter one another; and a great sword was given him.” (Revelation 6:4) Now, mankind has been fighting wars for thousands of years. Why, then, should these words have a special significance for our day?

8 Remember that war on its own is not the sign of Jesus’ presence. The sign is made up of *all* the details of Jesus’ prophecy happening in the same general time period. But war is the first feature mentioned, so we might expect that this feature would be fulfilled in an outstanding way that would catch our attention. And everyone must admit that the wars of this 20th century are unparalleled in all previous history.

9 For example, no earlier wars—cruel and destructive as many were—came even close in destructiveness to the two world wars of the 20th century. Why, the first world war eventually caused about 14 million fatalities, more than the entire

---

8. Why would we expect *war* to be an outstanding feature of the sign?

9, 10. How did the prophecies regarding war begin to be fulfilled?

population of many countries. Truly, "there was granted to take peace away from the earth so that they should slaughter one another."

[10] According to the prophecy, "a great sword was given" to the warlike second horseman of the Apocalypse. How does that apply? In this: Weapons of war became far more deadly. Equipped with the tank, the airplane, deadly poison gas, submarines, and artillery that could fire explosive shells over several miles, man became more efficient in killing his neighbor. And since the first world war the "great sword" has become even more destructive—owing to the use of such things as radio communications, radar, sophisticated rifles, bacteriological and chemical weapons, flamethrowers, napalm, new types of bombs, intercontinental ballistic missiles, nuclear submarines, advanced airplanes, and huge battleships.

"A Beginning of Pangs of Distress"

[11] The early verses of Jesus' prophecy conclude with the words: "These things are a beginning of pangs of distress." This was certainly true of the first world war. Its end in 1918 did not bring peace for long. It was soon followed by limited but vicious mil-

11, 12. In what way was the first world war merely "a beginning of pangs of distress"?

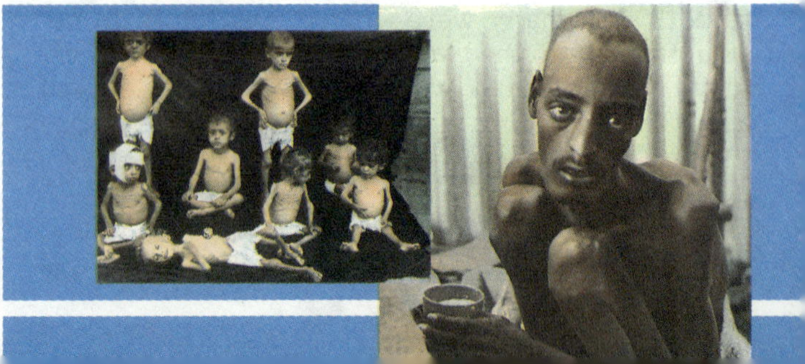

itary actions in Ethiopia, Libya, Spain, Russia, India, and other lands. Then came the horrendous second world war, which claimed some 50 million military and civilian victims.

12 Moreover, despite periodic peace agreements and lulls in the fighting, mankind is still at war. In 1987 it was reported that 81 major wars had been fought since 1960, killing 12,555,000 men, women, and children. The year 1987 saw more wars being fought than any previous year in recorded history.[1] Further, military preparation and expenditures, now reaching a total of about $1,000,000,000,000 annually, distort the economy of the world.[2] Jesus' prophecy of 'nation rising against nation and kingdom against kingdom' is surely undergoing fulfillment. The red horse of war continues its ferocious ride through the earth. But what about the second aspect of the sign?

Food Shortages!

13 Jesus foretold: "And there will be food shortages . . . in one place after another." Notice how this harmonizes with the ride of the third of the four horsemen of the Apocalypse. Of him we read: "I saw, and, look! a black horse; and the one seated upon it had a pair of scales in his hand. And I heard a voice as if in the midst of the four living creatures say: 'A quart of wheat for a denarius, and three quarts of barley for a denarius; and do not harm the olive oil and the wine.'" (Revelation 6:5, 6) Yes, severe food shortages!

---

13. What tragic events did Jesus foretell, and how did the vision of the third horseman of the Apocalypse support his prophecy?

14 Is it possible that this prophecy is being fulfilled today, when some lands have achieved such high standards of living? A glance at the world as a whole leaves no doubt as to the answer. Historically, famines have been caused by wars and natural disasters. It is not surprising, then, that our century, which has had more than its share of disasters and wars, has been plagued repeatedly with famines. Many parts of the earth have suffered such disasters since 1914. One report lists more than 60 major famines since 1914, in such widely separated lands as Greece, the Netherlands, the U.S.S.R., Nigeria, Chad, Chile, Peru, Bangladesh, Bengal, Kampuchea, Ethiopia, and Japan.[3] Some of these famines have lasted several years and caused millions of deaths.

15 Although severe famines usually get wide publicity, after a while they pass and survivors gradually return to a comparatively normal life. However, another more ominous type of food shortage has developed during the 20th century. This is less dramatic and therefore often ignored. But it persists year after year. This is a severe scourge of malnutrition that affects up to one fifth of the population of our planet and kills between 13 and 18 million people each year.[4]

16 In other words, this kind of food shortage regularly kills about as many people in two days as were killed at Hiroshima by the atom bomb. Indeed, every two years, there are more people who die from the effects of hunger than there were soldiers killed by World War I and World War II combined. Have

---

14. What major famines since 1914 have fulfilled Jesus' prophecy?
15, 16. What other food shortages are truly devastating today?

there been "food shortages . . . in one place after another" since 1914? Yes, indeed!

Earthquakes

17 On January 13, 1915, when the first world war was just a few months old, an earthquake shook Abruzzi, Italy, and took the lives of 32,610 people. This major disaster reminds us that wars and food shortages during Jesus' presence would be accompanied by something else: "There will be . . . earthquakes in one place after another." As with war and famine, the Abruzzi earthquake was just "a beginning of pangs of distress."*

18 The 20th century has been a century of earthquakes, and thanks to the development of the news media, all mankind is very much aware of the devastation they have caused. To mention just a few, 1920 saw 200,000 die in an earthquake in China; in 1923,

* There were at least five earthquakes between 1914 and 1918 that registered 8 or more on the Richter scale—more powerful than the earthquake at Abruzzi. However, these temblors were in remote areas of the globe, and thus they did not attract as much attention as the Italian quake.[5]

17. What devastating earthquake took place soon after 1914?
18. How has Jesus' prophecy regarding earthquakes been fulfilled?

some 99,300 died in a quake in Japan; in 1935, another quake killed 25,000 in what is now Pakistan, while 32,700 died in Turkey in 1939. There were 66,800 fatalities in an earthquake in Peru in 1970. And in 1976, some 240,000 (or, according to some sources, 800,000) died in Tangshan, China. More recently, in 1988, there were 25,000 who died in a powerful earthquake in Armenia.* Surely, "earthquakes in one place after another"![6]

"Deadly Plague"

19 Another detail of Jesus' prophecy has to do with disease. The evangelist Luke, in his account, records that Jesus foretold "in one place after another pestilences." (Luke 21:11) This too harmonizes with the prophetic vision of the four horsemen of the Apocalypse. The fourth horseman is named Death. He pictures premature death from a number of causes, including "deadly plague and . . . the wild beasts of the earth."—Revelation 6:8.

20 Back in 1918 and 1919, more than 1,000,000,000 people fell sick with Spanish influenza, and more than 20,000,000 died. The disease took more lives than did the great war itself.[7] And "deadly plague," or 'pestilence,' continues to afflict this generation, despite many remarkable medical advances. Why is this? For one thing, poorer lands do not always enjoy the benefits of scientific progress. Poor people suffer

---

* Varying figures have been reported for the number of victims of some of these disasters. All, however, were extremely destructive.

---

19. What further detail of the sign was foretold by Jesus and foreshadowed by the fourth horseman of the Apocalypse?

20. What outstanding epidemic was a partial fulfillment of Jesus' prophecy about pestilences?

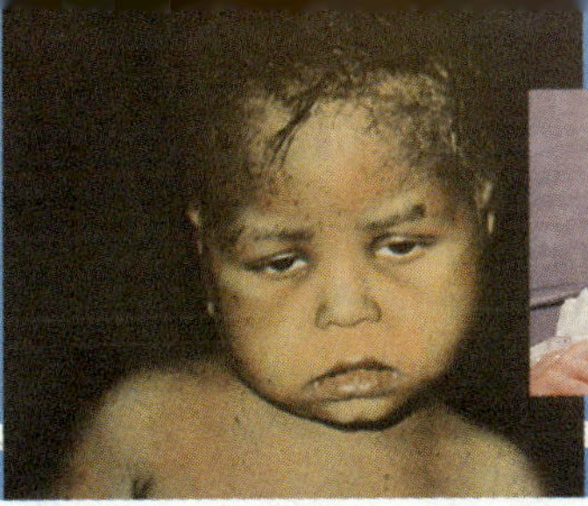
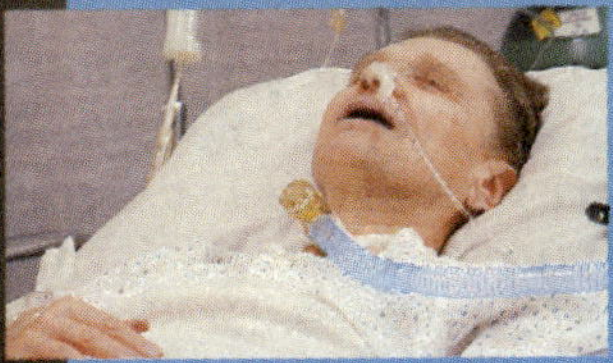

and die of sicknesses that could be cured if more money would be made available.

[21] Thus, some 150 million people worldwide suffer from malaria. Some 200 million are infected with snail fever. Chagas' disease afflicts about ten million people. About 40 million suffer from river blindness. Acute diarrheic diseases kill millions of children each year.[8] Tuberculosis and leprosy are still a significant health problem. Outstandingly, the poor of this world suffer from 'pestilences in one place after another.'

[22] But so do the wealthy. Influenza, for example, afflicts rich and poor alike. In 1957 one strain of influenza caused 70,000 deaths in the United States alone. In Germany it is estimated that one person in six will eventually suffer from cancer.[9] Sexually transmitted diseases also strike the wealthy and the poor. Gonorrhea, the most frequently reported communicable disease in the United States, afflicts as many as 18.9 percent of the population of some parts of Africa.[10] Syphilis, chlamydia, and genital herpes are some of the other pandemic sexually transmitted "pestilences."

21, 22. How have people in both rich lands and poor lands suffered from "deadly plague"?

23 In recent years, the "deadly plague" of AIDS has also joined the list of "pestilences." AIDS is a terrifying illness because, as of this writing, there is no cure in sight, and the number of its victims continues to increase. Dr. Jonathan Mann, director of the WHO (World Health Organization) Special Program on AIDS, said: "We also estimate that there are five to 10 million people in the world today infected with the human immunodeficiency virus (HIV)."[11] According to one published estimate, the AIDS virus strikes a new victim each minute. "Deadly plague" indeed! But what about the prophecy of death by wild beasts?

"The Wild Beasts of the Earth"

24 The fact is, when wild beasts are mentioned these days in the newspapers, it is because certain species are endangered or nearly extinct. "The wild beasts of the earth" are far more threatened by humans than humans are by them. Despite this, in some lands wild animals, such as tigers in India, still take a steady toll of human lives.

25 The Bible, however, draws our attention to another kind of wild beast that has caused real fear in recent years. The prophet Ezekiel compared violent men to wild animals when he said: "Her princes in the midst of her are like wolves tearing prey in shedding blood, in destroying souls for the purpose of making unjust gain." (Ezekiel 22:27) When he prophesied an "increasing of lawlessness," Jesus, in

---

23. What "deadly plague" has recently captured the headlines?
24, 25. (a) To what kind of 'wild beast' did the prophet Ezekiel refer? (b) What did Jesus say about "wild beasts" being active on earth during his presence?

effect, was saying that such "wild beasts" would be active on earth during his presence. (Matthew 24: 12) The Bible writer Paul adds that during "the last days" men would be "lovers of money . . . without self-control, fierce, without love of goodness." (2 Timothy 3:1-3) Has such been the case since 1914?

[26] It certainly has. If you live in almost any big city on earth, you already know this. But if you doubt it, just consider the following recent newspaper quotations. From Colombia: "Last year the police recorded . . . about 10,000 murders and 25,000 armed robberies." From Victoria, Australia: "Big Jump in Major Crime." From the United States: "Slayings in New York Heading for a Record High." "Detroit overtook Gary, Ind., last year as the major city with the highest murder rate in the nation—58 per 100,000 inhabitants."

[27] From Zimbabwe: "Infant murders have assumed crisis proportions." From Brazil: "There is so much crime here, and so much toting of weapons, that news of violence just doesn't generate much excitement anymore." From New Zealand: "Sexual attacks and violent crime continue to be a major concern for police." "New Zealanders' level of violence towards each other could only be described as barbaric." From Spain: "Spain grapples with growing crime problem." From Italy: "Sicilian Mafia, after setback, revives in wave of killings."

[28] These are just a small sample of newspaper

26-28. What reports from around the world show that criminal "wild beasts" are prowling the earth?

reports appearing shortly before the publication of this book. Surely, "wild beasts" are prowling the earth, causing people to tremble for their safety.

Preaching the Good News

29 How would religion fare during the troubled time of Jesus' presence? On the one hand, Jesus prophesied that there would be an increase in religious activity: "Many false prophets will arise and mislead many." (Matthew 24:11) On the other hand, he foretold that in Christendom as a whole, interest in God would be at a low ebb. "The love of the greater number will cool off."—Matthew 24:12.

30 This truly describes what is happening today in Christendom. On the one hand, mainstream churches everywhere are failing through lack of support. In the once strongly Protestant lands of northern Europe and England, religion is all but dead. At the same time, the Catholic Church is suffering from a lack of priests and from shrinking support. On the other hand, there have been surges in fringe religious elements. Cults based on Eastern religions proliferate, while greedy television evangelists extort millions of dollars.

29, 30. What is the religious situation in Christendom, in fulfillment of Jesus' prophecy?

31 What, though, about true Christianity, the religion introduced by Jesus and preached by his apostles? It would still exist during Jesus' presence, but how would it be recognized? There are a number of things that identify true Christianity, and one is mentioned in Jesus' great prophecy. True Christians would be occupied in a worldwide preaching work. Jesus prophesied: "And this good news of the kingdom will be preached in all the inhabited earth for a witness to all the nations; and then the end will come."—Matthew 24:14.

32 This preaching is now taking place on a colossal scale! Today, the religious group called Jehovah's Witnesses is engaged in the most intensive preaching activity in the history of Christianity. (Isaiah 43:10, 12) Back in 1919, while Christendom's politically minded major religions were advocating the ill-fated League of Nations, Jehovah's Witnesses were being prepared for this global preaching campaign.

33 There were only about 10,000 Witnesses back then, but they knew the work that had to be done. Courageously, they set about the task of preaching. They realized that a clergy-laity division was contrary to both the Bible's commands and the apostolic pattern. So all of them, to the last individual, learned how to speak to their neighbors about God's Kingdom. They became an organization of preachers.

34 As time went on, these preachers endured

---

31. What did Jesus foretell that helps identify true Christians today?

32. What group alone has fulfilled Jesus' prophecy recorded in Matthew 24:14?

33, 34. To what extent has the good news of the Kingdom been preached throughout the world?

intense opposition. In Europe, they were opposed by different kinds of totalitarian regimes. In the United States and Canada, they faced up to legal challenges and mob action. In other lands, they had to overcome fanatical religious prejudice and ruthless persecution by tyrannical dictators. In recent years, they have also had to counter the spirit of skepticism and self-indulgence that has developed. But they have persevered to the point where, today, there are more than three and a half million of them in 212 lands. Never before has the good news of the Kingdom been preached so widely—a striking fulfillment of this aspect of the sign!

What Does It All Mean?

35 Without any doubt we are witnessing the fulfillment of the great sign that Jesus gave. This fact adds to the evidence that the Bible is indeed inspired by God. No human could have foretold so long in advance the events that would take place during this 20th century. Moreover, the fulfillment of the sign means that we are living in the time of Jesus' presence and of the conclusion of the system of things. (Matthew 24:3) What is the significance of this? What is involved in Jesus' presence? And what is the system of things that is concluding? To answer these questions, we need to consider another strong evidence of the inspiration of the Bible: its remarkable internal harmony. We will discuss this next and see how the Bible's major theme is even now approaching an awe-inspiring climax.

---

35. (a) How does the fulfillment of prophecy today help to demonstrate the divine inspiration of the Bible? (b) What does the fulfillment of the sign that Jesus gave mean for our day?

Chapter 11

The Overall Harmony of the Bible

Imagine a library of 66 books written by about 40 different people over a period of 1,600 years. Three languages were used by writers who lived in a number of lands. All the writers had different personalities, abilities, and backgrounds. But when the books they wrote were eventually gathered together, it turned out that, really, they made up just one great book following one basic theme from beginning to end. That is hard to imagine, is it not? Yet, the Bible is just such a library.

NO HONEST student can fail to be impressed by the fact that the Bible, although a collection of different books, is one unified production. It is unified in that, from beginning to end, it promotes worship of just one God whose characteristics never change, and all its books develop one overriding theme. This overall harmony is powerful evidence that the Bible is, indeed, the Word of God.

2 The basic theme of the Bible is introduced in the

---

1. (Include introduction.) What remarkable harmony testifies to the fact that the Bible is inspired by God?

2, 3. What prophecy uttered in Eden gave a basis for hope, and what circumstances led to the uttering of that prophecy?

earliest chapters of its very first book, Genesis. There, we read that our first parents, Adam and Eve, were created perfect and placed in a paradise garden, Eden. Eve, however, was approached by a serpent that challenged the rightness of God's laws and lured her with subtle lies into a course of sin. Adam followed her and also disobeyed God. The result? Both were expelled from Eden and were condemned to death. We today suffer from the results of that first rebellion. We all inherit sin and death from our first parents.—Genesis 3:1-7, 19, 24; Romans 5:12.

3 At that tragic time, however, God uttered a prophecy that gave a basis for hope. The prophecy was spoken to the serpent, but it was uttered in the hearing of Adam and Eve so that they could tell it to their children. Here is what God said: "And I shall put enmity between you and the woman and between your seed and her seed. He will bruise you in the head and you will bruise him in the heel."—Genesis 3:15; Romans 8:20, 21.

4 Notice the four entities that are mentioned in this theme verse: the serpent and its seed as well as the woman and her seed. These entities would be key players in events for thousands of years to come. Constant enmity was to exist between the woman and her seed on the one hand and the serpent and his seed on the other. This enmity would include the ongoing conflict between true worship and false, right conduct and wickedness. At one stage, the serpent would gain a seeming advantage when it bruised the heel of the woman's seed. Eventually, though, the

---

4. What entities were mentioned in Jehovah's prophecy in Eden, and how would they interact through the centuries?

The Bible's first prophecy gave fallen mankind a basis for hope

woman's seed was to crush the serpent's head, and God himself would be vindicated when all traces of that original rebellion were removed.

5 Who are the woman and the serpent? And who are their seeds? When Eve had her first son, Cain, she exclaimed: "I have produced a man with the aid of Jehovah." (Genesis 4:1) Perhaps she felt that she was the woman of the prophecy and that this son would prove to be the seed. Cain, however, had a bad spirit like that of the serpent. He turned out to be a murderer, killing his own younger brother Abel. (Genesis 4:8) Clearly, the prophecy had a deeper, symbolic meaning that only God could explain. And this he did, a little at a time. All 66 books of the Bible contribute in one way or another to the revelation of the meaning of this, the first prophecy in the Bible.

Who Is the Serpent?

6 First, who is the serpent spoken about in Genesis 3:15? The account says that a literal serpent approached Eve in Eden, but literal serpents cannot speak. There must have been some power behind

---

5. How do we know that Eve was not the woman of the prophecy?
6-8. What words of Jesus help us to identify the power behind the serpent? Explain.

that snake, causing it to do what it did. What was that power? It was not until the first century of our Common Era, when Jesus was performing his ministry here on earth, that the identity of that power was clearly revealed.

[7] On one occasion, Jesus was speaking with some self-righteous Jewish religious leaders who boasted that they were sons of Abraham. Yet, they had adamantly opposed the truth preached by Jesus. So Jesus said to them: "You are from your father the Devil, and you wish to do the desires of your father. That one was a manslayer when he began, and he did not stand fast in the truth, because truth is not in him. When he speaks the lie, he speaks according to his own disposition, because he is a liar and the father of the lie."—John 8:44.

[8] Jesus' words were strong and to the point. He described the Devil as "a manslayer" and "the father of the lie." Now, the very first recorded lies were those spoken by the serpent in Eden. Whoever spoke those lies was indeed "the father of the lie." Moreover, those lies resulted in the death of Adam and Eve, making that ancient liar a murderer. Obviously, then, the power behind the serpent in Eden was Satan the Devil, and Jehovah was really talking to Satan in that ancient prophecy.

[9] Some have asked: If God is good, why did he create such a creature as the Devil? Jesus' words also help us to answer that question. Jesus said of Satan: "[He] was a manslayer *when he began.*" So when Satan lied to Eve, that was when he began to be

---

9. How did Satan come into existence?

Satan—from a Hebrew word that means "resister." God did not create Satan. A previously faithful angel allowed wrong desire to develop in his heart so that he *became* Satan.—Deuteronomy 32:4; compare Job 1:6-12; 2:1-10; James 1:13-15.

The Seed of the Serpent

10 What, though, of 'the seed [or offspring] of the serpent'? Jesus' words also help us to solve this part of the puzzle. He said to the Jewish religious leaders: "You are from your father the Devil, *and you wish to do the desires of your father.*" These Jews were descendants of Abraham, just as they boasted. But their wicked conduct made them spiritual children of Satan, the originator of sin.

11 The apostle John, writing toward the end of the first century, explains clearly who belong to the seed of the Serpent, Satan. He writes: "He who carries on sin originates with the Devil, because the Devil has been sinning from the beginning. . . . The children of God and the children of the Devil are evident by this fact: Everyone who does not carry on righteousness does not originate with God, neither does he who does not love his brother." (1 John 3:8, 10) Evidently, the seed of the Serpent have been very active throughout all human history!

Who Is the Seed of the Woman?

12 Who, then, is 'the seed [or offspring] of the woman'? This is one of the most important questions

---

10, 11. How do Jesus and the apostle John help us to identify the Serpent's seed?

12, 13. (a) How did Jehovah reveal to Abraham that the woman's seed would appear among his descendants? (b) Who inherited the promise concerning the Seed?

ever asked, for it is the woman's seed that will eventually crush the head of Satan and undo the evil effects of the original rebellion. Back in the 20th century B.C.E., God revealed a major clue about this one's identity to the faithful man Abraham. Because of Abraham's great faith, God made a series of promises to him about the offspring that would be born to him. One of these made it evident that 'the woman's seed' that would 'bruise the serpent's head' was going to appear among Abraham's children. God told him: "Your seed will take possession of the gate of his enemies. And by means of your seed all nations of the earth will certainly bless themselves due to the fact that you have listened to my voice."—Genesis 22: 17, 18.

13 As the years went by, Jehovah's promise to Abraham was repeated to Abraham's son Isaac and to his grandson Jacob. (Genesis 26:3-5; 28:10-15) Eventually, Jacob's descendants became 12 tribes, and one of those tribes, Judah, received a special promise: "The scepter will not turn aside from Judah, neither the commander's staff from between his feet, until Shiloh comes; and to him the obedience of the peoples will belong." (Genesis 49:10) Evidently, the Seed was to appear in the tribe of Judah.

14 At the end of the 16th century B.C.E., the

---

14. What nation was organized to be prepared for the coming of the Seed?

In the 20th century B.C.E., Jehovah told Abraham that the promised Seed would come from among his descendants

In the 11th century B.C.E., King David learned that the Seed would come from his royal line

12 tribes of Israel were organized into a nation as God's special people. To this end, God made a solemn covenant with them and gave them a law code. The main reason for this was to prepare a people for the coming of the Seed. (Exodus 19:5, 6; Galatians 3:24) From then on, the enmity of Satan toward the woman's Seed was seen in the hostility of the nations to God's chosen people.

15 The final clue as to which family would produce the Seed was given in the 11th century B.C.E. At that time, God spoke to the second king of Israel, David, and promised that the Seed would come from his line and that this One's throne would be "firmly established to time indefinite." (2 Samuel 7:11-16) From that point on, the Seed could properly be referred to as the son of David.—Matthew 22:42-45.

16 In the years that followed, God raised up prophets to give more inspired information about the coming Seed. For example, in the eighth century B.C.E., Isaiah wrote: "There has been a child born to us, there has been a son given to us; and the princely rule will come to be upon his shoulder. And his name will be called Wonderful Counselor, Mighty God,

---

15. What final clue was given as to which family among Abraham's descendants would produce the Seed?

16, 17. How did Isaiah describe the blessings the Seed would bring?

Eternal Father, Prince of Peace. To the abundance of the princely rule and to peace there will be no end, upon the throne of David and upon his kingdom." —Isaiah 9:6, 7.

17 Isaiah further prophesied about this Seed: "With righteousness he must judge the lowly ones, and with uprightness he must give reproof in behalf of the meek ones of the earth. . . . And the wolf will actually reside for a while with the male lamb, and with the kid the leopard itself will lie down, and the calf and the maned young lion and the well-fed animal all together . . . They will not do any harm or cause any ruin in all my holy mountain; because the earth will certainly be filled with the knowledge of Jehovah as the waters are covering the very sea." (Isaiah 11:4-9) What rich blessings this seed was going to bring!

18 In the sixth century before our Common Era, Daniel recorded a further prophecy about the Seed. He foretold the time when one like a son of man would appear in heaven and said that "to him there were given rulership and dignity and kingdom, that the peoples, national groups and languages should all serve even him." (Daniel 7:13, 14) So the coming Seed would inherit a heavenly kingdom, and his royal authority would extend over all the earth.

---

18. What further information about the Seed did Daniel record?

In the eighth century B.C.E., Isaiah foretold the blessings the Seed would bring

In the sixth century B.C.E., Daniel foretold that the Seed would rule in a heavenly kingdom

The Puzzle Solved

19 The identity of the Seed was finally unveiled at the dawn of our Common Era. In the year 2 B.C.E., an angel appeared to a young Jewish girl named Mary, who was a descendant of David. The angel told her that she was going to give birth to a very special baby and said: "This one will be great and will be called Son of the Most High; and Jehovah God will give him the throne of David his father, and he will rule as king over the house of Jacob forever, and there will be no end of his kingdom." (Luke 1:32, 33) So the long wait for the "seed" was finally coming to an end.

20 In the year 29 C.E. (a date pointed to long in advance by Daniel), Jesus was baptized. Holy spirit then descended upon him, and God acknowledged him as his Son. (Daniel 9:24-27; Matthew 3:16, 17) For three and a half years thereafter, Jesus witnessed to the Jews, proclaiming: "The kingdom of the heavens has drawn near." (Matthew 4:17) During that time, he fulfilled so many prophecies from the Hebrew Scriptures that there was no room for doubt that he was indeed the promised Seed.

---

19. What role, as revealed by the angel, was Mary to play in the coming of the Seed?

20. Who is the promised Seed, and what message did he preach in Israel?

21 The early Christians understood this well. Paul explained to the Christians in Galatia: "Now the promises were spoken to Abraham and to his seed. It says, not: 'And to seeds,' as in the case of many such, but as in the case of one: 'And to your seed,' who is Christ." (Galatians 3:16) Jesus was to be the "Prince of Peace" foretold by Isaiah. After he would finally come into his Kingdom, justice and righteousness would be established worldwide.

Who, Then, Is the Woman?

22 If Jesus is the Seed, who is the woman who was referred to back there in Eden? Since the power behind the serpent was a spirit creature, we should not be surprised that the woman too is spirit and not human. The apostle Paul spoke about a heavenly "woman" when he said: "But the Jerusalem above is free, and she is our mother." (Galatians 4:26) Other scriptures indicate that this "Jerusalem above" had already existed for millenniums. She is Jehovah's heavenly organization of spirit creatures, from which Jesus descended to fulfill the role of 'the seed of the woman.' Only this kind of spiritual "woman" could endure the enmity of "the original serpent" for millenniums.—Revelation 12:9; Isaiah 54:1, 13; 62:2-6.

23 This brief overview of the development of that ancient prophecy in Genesis 3:15 is a powerful testimony to the grand harmony of the Bible. It is truly remarkable that the prophecy can be understood

---

21. What did the early Christians understand as to the identity of the Seed?
22. Who is the woman referred to in Jehovah's prophecy in Eden?
23. Why is the progressive revealing of the meaning of Jehovah's Edenic prophecy so remarkable?

Near the beginning of the first century C.E., Mary learned that Jesus, the baby she was to bear, would grow up to be the Seed

only when we put the events and sayings from the 20th, the 11th, the 8th, and the 6th centuries B.C.E. together with the sayings and events from the first century of our Common Era. This cannot have happened by chance. There must have been a guiding hand behind it all.—Isaiah 46:9, 10.

The Meaning for Us

24 What does all of this mean for us? Well, Jesus is the primary 'seed of the woman.' That ancient prophecy in Genesis 3:15 foretold that his heel would be 'bruised' by the Serpent, and this happened when Jesus died on the torture stake. A bruise is not lasting. Thus, the Serpent's seeming success was quickly turned into defeat when Jesus was resurrected. (As we saw in Chapter 6, there is overwhelming evidence that this really occurred.) Jesus' death became the basis for the salvation of righthearted mankind, so the Seed began to be a blessing, just as God had promised Abraham. But what about the prophecies that Jesus was to rule from a heavenly kingdom over all his earthly realm?

---

24. What does the identification of the Seed mean for us?

25 In a graphic prophetic vision recorded in Revelation chapter 12, the beginning of this Kingdom is pictured as the birth of a male child in heaven. In this Kingdom, the promised Seed takes power under the title Michael, meaning "Who Is Like God?" He shows that no one can rightfully challenge Jehovah's sovereignty, when he casts "the original serpent" out of heaven for all time. We read: "So down the great dragon was hurled, the original serpent, the one called Devil and Satan, who is misleading the entire inhabited earth; he was hurled down to the earth." —Revelation 12:7-9.

26 The result is relief for the heavens but distress on earth. "Now have come to pass the salvation and the power and the kingdom of our God and the authority of his Christ," came the triumphant shout. Furthermore, we read: "On this account be glad, you heavens and you who reside in them! Woe for the earth and for the sea, because the Devil has come down to you, having great anger, knowing he has a short period of time."—Revelation 12:10, 12.

27 Can we say when this prophecy was to be fulfilled? Really, that was the question raised by the disciples when they asked Jesus about 'the sign of his presence and of the conclusion of the system of things'—as we discussed in Chapter 10. (Matthew 24:3) As we saw, the evidence is overwhelming that Jesus' presence in heavenly Kingdom power began in 1914. Since that time, we have experienced "woe for the earth" indeed!

25, 26. What issue was involved in the enmity between 'the seed of the woman' and the Serpent, as described in Revelation?
27. When was the prophecy about Satan's being cast from the heavens fulfilled? How do we know?

28 But notice: That heavenly cry announced that Satan has only "a short period of time." So that original prophecy in Genesis 3:15 is moving to its unerring climax. The serpent, his seed, the woman, and her seed have all been identified. The Seed was 'bruised in the heel,' but he recovered. Soon, the crushing of Satan (and his seed) will begin under God's now-reigning King, Christ Jesus.

29 This will involve tremendous changes on the earthly scene. Along with Satan, those who prove themselves to be his seed will be removed. As the psalmist prophesied: "Just a little while longer, and the wicked one will be no more; and you will certainly give attention to his place, and he will not be." (Psalm 37:10) What a radical change *that* will be! Then, the psalmist's further words will be fulfilled: "But the meek ones themselves will possess the earth, and they will indeed find their exquisite delight in the abundance of peace."—Psalm 37:11.

30 In this way, the "Prince of Peace" will finally bring peace to mankind. This is the promise of the Bible, as we noted at Isaiah 9:6, 7. In this skeptical age, many find such a promise unrealistic. But what alternative does man offer? None! On the other hand, this promise is clearly stated in the Bible, and the Bible is the unfailing Word of God. It is really the skeptics who are unrealistic. (Isaiah 55:8, 11) They ignore God, who inspired the Bible and who is the greatest reality of all.

28, 29. What great changes on the earthly scene still lie ahead, and how do we know they will take place soon?
30. Why are skeptics who cast doubt on the inspiration of the Bible and even on God's existence the unrealistic ones?

Chapter 12

A Higher Source of Wisdom

"How many your works are, O Jehovah! All of them in wisdom you have made. The earth is full of your productions." (*Psalm 104:24*) *Yes, from the magnificence of the vast universe to the delicate beauty of a flower, creation testifies to the matchless wisdom of its Creator. The technology of this 20th century pales into insignificance when compared with God's works. If the Bible is God's Word, we would also expect it to give evidence of wisdom that is beyond human capabilities. Does it?*

THE Bible stresses the importance of wisdom. It says: "Wisdom is the prime thing. Acquire wisdom; and with all that you acquire, acquire understanding." (Proverbs 4:7) It also acknowledges that we humans often lack wisdom, and it encourages us: "If any one of you is lacking in wisdom, let him keep on asking God, for he gives generously to all." —James 1:5.

2 How does God 'give wisdom generously'? One way is by encouraging us to read the Bible and learn from it. The Bible book of Proverbs urges:

---

1. (Include introduction.) (a) Where do we see evidence of God's matchless wisdom? (b) What counsel does the Bible give regarding wisdom?
2. How can a person increase his wisdom?

Walking with wise persons makes us wise, but associating with stupid persons will affect us badly

"My son, if you will receive my sayings and treasure up my own commandments with yourself, so as to pay attention to wisdom . . . you will understand the fear of Jehovah, and you will find the very knowledge of God. For Jehovah himself gives wisdom." (Proverbs 2:1, 2, 5, 6) When we apply the counsel in the Bible and see how effective it is, we realize that it truly represents divine wisdom.

Wise Sayings

[3] To appreciate this better, let us look at a few Bible verses. Consider this wise saying: "Those who are determined to be rich fall into temptation and a snare and many senseless and hurtful desires . . . For the love of money is a root of all sorts of injurious things." (1 Timothy 6:9, 10) Compare this with the modern viewpoint—at least in Western society—that encourages people to pursue money as their prime goal. Unhappily, many gain the wealth they seek and still have a feeling of emptiness and dissatisfaction. A clinical psychologist noted: "Becoming No. 1 and rich does not make you feel fulfilled, satisfied, authentically respected or loved."[1]

3, 4. (a) What does the Bible say as to the vanity of the love of money? (b) What fine balance does the Bible display in counseling us on the value of money?

4 Not that a practical person can completely turn his back on money. The Bible shows a finely balanced wisdom when it says: "Wisdom is for a protection the same as money is for a protection; but the advantage of knowledge is that wisdom itself preserves alive its owners." (Ecclesiastes 7:12) Thus, the Bible helps us to see that money, while important, is not all-important. It is only a means to an end, and it is of limited value if we do not have the wisdom to use it properly.

5 This Bible statement is also true: "He that is walking with wise persons will become wise, but he that is having dealings with the stupid ones will fare badly." (Proverbs 13:20) Have you ever noticed what a powerful effect our associates have on us? Peer pressure has led young people into drunkenness, drug abuse, and immorality. If we mix with those who use foul language, we eventually find ourselves using foul language. Keeping company with dishonest individuals tends to make us dishonest. Truly, as the Bible also says, "Bad associations spoil useful habits."—1 Corinthians 15:33.

6 On the other hand, good associations can improve us. By "walking with wise persons," we will become wiser ourselves. Good habits rub off, just as bad ones do. Once again, the Bible shows wisdom in encouraging us to choose our associates carefully.

7 The Bible has many such precepts to help us guide our lives. As a source of advice, it is unique. Its counsel is *always* beneficial. It is never merely

---

5, 6. (a) Why is the Bible counsel to avoid bad associations wise? (b) How do we benefit from "walking with wise persons"?
7. What makes the Bible unique as a source of advice?

Smoking tobacco is to be avoided because it is against Bible principles

theoretical, and it never works to our harm. The wide range of Bible counsel is unequaled. Those who apply it in their lives, and see how it always works out for their good, come to appreciate the Bible as a unique source of wisdom.

Wise Principles

8 What, though, if we face a situation that is not specifically mentioned in the Bible? Often, we find broad principles to guide us. For example, many at some time in their lives face a decision regarding the habit of smoking tobacco. Since tobacco was unknown in the Middle East in Jesus' days, the Bible does not mention it. Nevertheless, there are appropriate Bible principles to help us make a wise decision in this matter.

9 Smoking tobacco, while reportedly pleasurable, actually involves inhaling concentrated pollutants into the lungs. A smoker pollutes his body, as well as his clothes and the air around him. In addition, smoking is an addiction. People who want

---

8. How can the Bible help us even when we face a situation not specifically mentioned in it?

9-11. In what way do Bible principles help us to come to a wise decision in the matter of using tobacco, and how do we benefit by following these principles?

to stop often find it very difficult. With this in mind, we can look to the Bible for help in reaching a wise conclusion about smoking tobacco.

10 First, consider the problem of addiction. Paul, when speaking about foods, said: "I will not let myself be brought under authority by anything." (1 Corinthians 6:12) Paul was free to eat any kind of food, but he knew that some people back there had sensitive consciences. So he said he was not so "addicted" to certain foods that he could not give them up if he had to in order to keep from stumbling others. If a person cannot stop smoking—or chewing—tobacco, he is definitely 'under its authority.' So Paul's statement on the matter of food is a good guideline for tobacco use. We should not allow ourselves to become enslaved by a habit.

11 Second, consider the matter of pollution. The Bible says: "Let us cleanse ourselves of every defilement of flesh and spirit." (2 Corinthians 7:1) Smoking is without doubt a defilement, or a pollution, of the flesh. The seriousness of this pollution is seen in the fact that, according to the World Health Organization, it causes more than a million people to die prematurely each year. If we follow the Bible principle about staying clean from defilements of the flesh, we will be protected from the serious health hazards of smoking, as well as drugs and other defilements.

Beneficial Words

12 We should not be surprised that following Bible counsel benefits us in a physical way. Bible

---

12. Why is Bible counsel always linked to our physical and emotional well-being?

counsel comes from God. As our Creator, he has an intimate knowledge of how we are made and what we need. (Psalm 139:14-16) His counsel is always linked to our physical and emotional well-being.

13 This is seen in the counsel not to tell lies. Lies are listed among the seven things that Jehovah hates, and the book of Revelation lists liars among those who will have no place in God's new world. (Proverbs 6:19; Revelation 21:8) In spite of this, lying is widespread. One business magazine notes: "The U.S. is experiencing the worst outbreak of fraud, deception and related abuses in its history."[2]

14 Common as it is, though, lying is bad for society and bad for the individual. Columnist Clifford Longley correctly notes: "Lies hurt the liar and the lied-to, at the profoundest level of their being, by severing that essential contact between mind and reality."[3] *The American Journal of Psychiatry* states: "The psychological impact on persons on the receiving end of lies can be devastating. Major life decisions may be based on false information believed to be correct. Lies may also have adverse effects on liars themselves."[4] How much better to tell the truth, as the Bible wisely counsels!

15 In a more positive vein, the Bible tells us that we should be concerned for others, show love for them, and be helpful to them. Jesus' words are well known: "All things, therefore, that you want men

---

13, 14. Why is it the course of wisdom to follow the Bible counsel not to tell lies?

15, 16. In what ways is it to our benefit to follow the Bible counsel to show love to others?

to do to you, you also must likewise do to them." —Matthew 7:12.

16 How much better the world would be if everyone followed this rule! Moreover, according to a psychological study conducted in the United States, individuals would *feel* better. The 1,700 people studied reported that helping others gave them a sense of calmness and relief from stress-related disorders such as headaches and voice loss. The report concludes: "It appears, then, that caring about others is as much a part of human nature as caring about ourselves."[5] This reminds us of the Bible command: "You must love your neighbor as yourself." (Matthew 22:39; compare John 13:34, 35.) It is natural to love ourselves. But for us to be emotionally healthy, the Bible says we have to balance that love for self with a love for others.

A helping attitude benefits everyone

Marriage and Morality

17 While Bible counsel gives evidence of deep wisdom, it does not always say the things people want to hear. Often, it is accused of being old-fashioned. Why is this? Because while the Bible's counsel is for our long-term good, applying it often takes discipline and self-denial; and these qualities are not popular today.

18 Take the matter of marriage and morality. The Bible's standards here are very strict. It specifies monogamy, one husband for one wife. And while it mentions extreme cases where divorce or

---

17. Why does Bible counsel sometimes appear old-fashioned?

18, 19. What are the Bible standards for marriage and morality?

separation might be possible, in general it says that the marriage bond is for life. "Did you not read that he who created them from the beginning made them male and female and said, 'For this reason a man will leave his father and his mother and will stick to his wife, and the two will be one flesh'? So that they are no longer two, but one flesh. Therefore, what God has yoked together let no man put apart."—Matthew 19:4-6; 1 Corinthians 7:12-15.

19 Moreover, the Bible says that the only place for sexual intimacy is within the marriage bond. It forbids all such intimacy outside marriage. We read: "Neither fornicators, nor idolaters, nor adulterers, nor men kept for unnatural purposes, nor men who lie with men . . . will inherit God's kingdom."—1 Corinthians 6:9, 10.

20 Today, these standards are widely ignored. Professor of sociology David Mace notes: "During the present century our culture has undergone extensive changes, and many ancient customs and institutions have been shaken to their foundations. Marriage has been no exception."[6] Loose moral practices are common. Sexual relations between teenage dating couples are often viewed as normal. Living together before marriage—'just to make sure'—is frequent. And once couples get married, illicit sexual affairs are not uncommon.

21 Has this looser moral climate brought happiness? No, it has brought nothing but turmoil—and

---

20. In what ways are Bible standards of morality being widely ignored today?

21. What has resulted from a widespread ignoring of Bible standards of marriage and morality?

expensive turmoil at that—resulting in unhappiness and broken homes. There is also a pandemic of sexually transmitted diseases directly traceable to loose morality. The spread of gonorrhea, syphilis, and chlamydia, among others, is out of control. In recent years, prostitution and homosexual practices have accelerated the spread of AIDS. There is an epidemic of young single girls having babies when they are hardly out of childhood themselves. *Ladies' Home Journal* noted: "The emphasis upon sex that typified the sixties and seventies has brought not infinite human happiness but some serious human misery."[7]

22 Hence, we now hear comments like the following by professor of sociology Carlfred B. Broderick: "Perhaps we are grown up enough to consider whether it would not serve us all better to promote premarital abstinence as a policy that is the most responsive to the needs of our citizens and their right to freedom: freedom from disease, freedom from unwanted pregnancy."[8] Truly, the Bible's standard of morality has proved, in the long run, to bring the greatest happiness.

Principles That Really Work

23 Since marriage is meant to last for life, we need to know how to make a success of it. Some have argued that it is better to get out of an unhappy marriage than to stay in it and be miserable. But there is another alternative: to work at solving the

---

22. In the matter of morality, what brings the greatest happiness?
23. (a) If a marriage is unhappy, is divorce the only possible solution? (b) What are two of the keys to a happy, stable marriage?

Those who follow Bible counsel in marriage have a solid basis for happiness

problems that are causing the unhappiness. This is another area where the Bible helps. We have already seen how it counsels us to be faithful to our marriage partner, and this is one key to a happy, stable marriage. Another is to recognize that there can be only one head in a marriage, and the Bible says it has to be the husband. The wife is counseled to be supportive of her husband and not challenge his position. The man, on the other hand, is told to use his position for the good of his wife and not be selfish.—1 Corinthians 11:3; 1 Timothy 2:11-14.

24 To the husband, the Bible says: "Husbands ought to be loving their wives as their own bodies. He who loves his wife loves himself, for no man ever hated his own flesh." (Ephesians 5:28, 29) The loving husband exercises his authority in a considerate way. He remembers that although he is the head, his wife should be considered and consulted. Marriage is a partnership, not a dictatorship.

25 Bible counsel for wives includes these words: "The wife should have deep respect for her husband." (Ephesians 5:33) She respects her husband because of his position, and her respect will be

---

24, 25. How does the Bible encourage husbands and wives to fulfill their proper roles in marriage?

evidenced by her being supportive of him, just as her husband's love will be evidenced by his being concerned for her. To many modern-thinking individuals, advice such as this is unacceptable. But partnerships that base their relationships on love and respect—as the Bible counsels—are always happy.

26 The fact that Bible counsel in this area really works is seen in an experience from the South Seas. A couple there, after ten years together, were convinced that their marriage was a failure. So they started planning to separate. Then the wife spoke with one of Jehovah's Witnesses. Together, she and the Witness studied the Bible's advice for married couples. The husband reports: "As my wife was learning the Bible principles, she made efforts to apply them in her life. In a few weeks' time, I started to notice some changes." Intrigued, he agreed to join his wife's study of the Bible and learned the Bible's counsel for married men. The result? He says: "Now we have found the basis for a really happy family life."

27 Coping with poverty is yet another area where the Bible's counsel has proved helpful. For example, smoking and drunkenness, which are both contrary to Bible principles, waste limited resources. (Proverbs 23:19-21) Further, the Bible recommends industriousness, as a hardworking person can more often find a way to feed his family than

---

26. Do the Scriptural standards for marriage really work? Illustrate.

27. The application of which Bible principles can help Christians who suffer economic poverty?

can a lazy one or one who gives in to despair. (Proverbs 6:6-11; 10:26) Moreover, heeding the advice against being "envious of those doing unrighteousness" keeps a person from resorting to such things as crime or gambling as ways to alleviate poverty. (Psalm 37:1) Such practices may seem to offer a quick solution to financial difficulties, but their long-term fruitage is very bitter.

28 Does this counsel really help those who are very poor, or is it just idealistic theory? The answer is, The advice works, as many experiences around the world show. To take just one example, a Christian woman in Asia found herself widowed, without any income, and with a young son to take care of. How did the Bible help her and her son?

29 She was industrious, as the Bible counsels, and started making clothes and selling them. Because she was honest and reliable, as the Bible also counsels, she soon had regular customers. (Colossians 3:23) Then, she converted a small room in her house into a small eating place and rose about four o'clock each morning to prepare food to sell, and

---

28-30. (a) How did applying Bible principles help one Christian woman to deal with poverty? (b) To what do the experiences of thousands of Christians in economically poor circumstances testify?

Applying Bible counsel helps people to cope with the severe problems of poverty

this added to her income. "Even so," she says, "we have to live simply." But she remembers the Bible advice: "Having sustenance and covering, we shall be content with these things."—1 Timothy 6:8.

30 She adds: "Although I live near the poverty line, I am not resentful or bitter. Bible truth fills me with a positive outlook." In addition, she has found that a notable promise that Jesus gave has really worked in her case. He said: "Keep on, then, seeking first the kingdom and his righteousness, and all these other things [material necessities] will be added to you." (Matthew 6:33) Her experience has been that by putting her service to God first in her life, she always receives, in one way or another, the material necessities. The experiences of this Christian lady, taken with those of countless other economically poor Christians, add to the testimony that the Bible's counsel really works.

31 In this chapter, we have merely touched on the vast wealth of counsel and advice that the Bible contains, and we have seen just a few cases where this counsel has worked. The experiences mentioned could be multiplied a thousandfold. Time and again, when people follow the Bible, they benefit. When they ignore it, they suffer. No other body of counsel, ancient or modern, is so *consistently* beneficial and applies to people of all races. Wise counsel such as this cannot be merely folk wisdom. The fact that the Bible is a rich repository of such wisdom is powerful evidence that it is the Word of God.

---

31. What happens when we follow Bible counsel, and to what does this fact bear witness?

Chapter 13

"The Word of God Is Alive"

In the previous chapter, we saw that Bible counsel can help us to solve problems and avoid mistakes. The timeless wisdom of the Bible's counsel is strong evidence of inspiration. The Bible itself says: "All Scripture is inspired of God and beneficial for teaching, for reproving, for setting things straight, for disciplining in righteousness." (2 Timothy 3:16) *But the Bible does more than give us wise counsel. As the Word of God, it actually changes people.*

CAN the Bible really change people? Yes, it can even alter their personality. Consider this counsel recorded in the Bible: "You should put away the old personality which conforms to your former course of conduct and which is being corrupted according to his deceptive desires; but . . . you should be made new in the force actuating your mind, and should put on the new personality which was created according to God's will in true righteousness and loyalty."—Ephesians 4:22-24.

2 Is it truly possible to put on a new personality? Yes, it is! In fact, becoming a Christian sometimes

---

1-3. (a) How does the Bible emphasize the need for personality changes? (b) What experience shows the power of the Bible to change personalities?

involves quite dramatic personality adjustments. (1 Corinthians 6:9-11) For example, a boy in South America was orphaned at the age of nine. Growing up without parental guidance, he developed severe personality problems. He relates: "By the time I was 18, I was completely addicted to drugs and had already spent time in prison for stealing to support the habit." His aunt, though, was one of Jehovah's Witnesses, and eventually she was able to help him.

3 He explains: "My aunt began to study the Bible with me, and after seven months I was able to break the drug habit." He also broke with his previous companions and made new friends among Jehovah's Witnesses. He goes on: "These new companions, along with my regular study of the Bible, enabled me to make progress and finally to dedicate my life to serve God." Yes, this former drug addict and thief became an active Christian, and this radical change was accomplished through the power of the Bible. Indeed, as the apostle Paul says, "The word of God is alive and exerts power."—Hebrews 4:12.

Changed Through Knowledge

4 How does the Bible change people? The answer is seen in this Bible passage: "Put them all away from you, wrath, anger, badness, abusive speech, and obscene talk out of your mouth. Do not be lying to one another. Strip off the old personality with its practices, and clothe yourselves with the new personality, which through accurate knowl-

---

4, 5. According to Colossians 3:8-10, what is needed in order to cultivate the new personality?

edge is being made new according to the image of the One who created it."—Colossians 3:8-10.

5 Notice the important part played by accurate knowledge of the Bible. The Bible explains which characteristics we need to get rid of and which we should cultivate. Such knowledge can in itself have a powerful effect, as a young man in southern Europe found. He had a real problem: a violent temper. While growing up, he was constantly in fights, and as an outlet for his violence, he took up boxing; but he still could not control his violent nature. When in the army, he got into trouble for beating a fellow soldier. After leaving the army, he got married but then beat his wife. In one family argument, he even beat his own father, knocking him to the ground. Truly an angry, violent young man!

The Bible actually changes people

6 Eventually, though, he studied the Bible with Jehovah's Witnesses and heard counsel such as the following: "Return evil for evil to no one. . . . If possible, as far as it depends upon you, be peaceable with all men. Do not avenge yourselves, beloved, but yield place to the wrath." (Romans 12:17-19) This helped him to realize how bad a weakness his violent temperament was. He gave up boxing, which he realized was not compatible with the peaceful Christian personality. But he still had a real struggle with his violent nature.

7 He was helped, however, by his increasing

6, 7. How did accurate knowledge of the Bible help a young man in southern Europe to change his personality?

knowledge of Bible principles. This refined his conscience, which in turn acted to counteract his quick temper. Once, after he had made some progress in his Bible studies, a stranger got angry and shouted insults at him. The young man felt the familiar rage welling up inside. Then, he felt another force: a sense of shame; and this prevented him from giving in to his anger. Rather than "return evil for evil," he controlled his spirit. Now, he is a changed person, with a new personality, thanks to accurate knowledge from the Bible.

Getting to Know God

8 True, many people know the right thing to do, but they give in to fleshly weaknesses. Clearly, simply having an accurate knowledge of right and wrong is not *all* that is needed. Something else helped the two individuals described above to change. What was it? The passage referred to earlier said: "Clothe yourselves with the new personality, which through accurate knowledge is being made new *according to the image of the One who created it."* (Colossians 3:10) Notice that, just as Adam was originally made in God's image, so the new personality is made in the image of God. (Genesis 1:26) Therefore, the accurate knowledge that helped these two young men had to include a knowledge of God. This reminds us of Jesus' words: "This means everlasting life, their taking in knowledge of you, the only true God, and of the one whom you sent forth, Jesus Christ."—John 17:3.

---

8. (a) In whose image is the new personality made? (b) The accurate knowledge that molds the new personality must include knowledge of whom?

9 How does a knowledge of God help us to change our personality? It gives us a motive to do so. When we come to know God through our study of the Bible, we learn of his divine qualities and see the love he has shown for us. This leads us to love him in return. (1 John 4:19) Then, we can obey what Jesus said was the first and greatest commandment: "You must love Jehovah your God with your whole heart and with your whole soul and with your whole mind." (Matthew 22:37) Loving God makes us *want* to put on the new personality that pleases him. It makes us want to be more like him, however hard we may have to struggle to do so.

Deeply Ingrained Weaknesses

10 In some cases, it really is a struggle. A young woman in North America had to fight very hard to change. A victim of childhood sexual abuse, she grew up in a violent family and eventually turned to drugs. Drugs were expensive, though, so she sold herself as a prostitute to pay for the habit. She also harassed and robbed tourists and ended up spending more time in prisons and poolrooms than she did at home.

11 When Jehovah's Witnesses met her, she had —after several abortions—become the mother of an illegitimate child. Nevertheless, she liked what she heard from the Bible and began to study it. Soon she was building a relationship with God and making adjustments in her life.

---

9. How does a knowledge of God help us to change our personality?

10, 11. How did accurate knowledge help a young North American woman to start to change her personality?

12 A hard fight lay ahead, however, because the old personality was deeply ingrained. On one occasion, she took offense at some well-meant counsel, quit studying the Bible, and went back to her unclean ways. But she could not forget the Bible truth that had been implanted in her, and she admits: "Every now and then I had feelings of guilt, and the words of 2 Peter 2:22 raced through my mind: 'The dog returns to its own vomit and the washed sow to the mire.'"

13 Eventually, this knowledge motivated her to make another determined effort. She says: "I began opening the door to Jehovah and praying often for help." This time, the new personality became more firmly implanted, although she still had to struggle hard. Once, in a moment of weakness, she relapsed into drunkenness and immorality. This time, though, her reaction showed that she was truly changing. She was disgusted with herself and says: "I did a lot of praying and studying." Eventually, God's Word exerted power in her life to such an extent that she became an active Christian, living a clean, honorable life. For several years now, she has been a totally different person from the abused, drug-addicted, wild-living individual that she used to be.

A People Changed by God's Word

14 The power that the Bible has wielded in the lives of humble individuals shows that it is more

---

12, 13. Describe how accurate knowledge, once implanted, acts as a force for change.

14, 15. (a) What force from God works through the Bible? (b) What are some characteristics of true Christians today?

than merely a human work. As the inspired Word of God, it is a channel for the operation of God's spirit. The same spirit that made possible the miracles Jesus performed helps us today to conquer bad qualities and develop a Christian personality. Indeed, the basic qualities that Christians need to cultivate—love, joy, peace, long-suffering, kindness, goodness, faith, mildness, and self-control—are called in the Bible "the fruitage of the spirit."—Galatians 5:22, 23.

A knowledge of God makes a person want to be like him

15 Today, this spirit is working not on just a few individuals but upon millions who have been "taught by Jehovah" and enjoy 'abundant peace' from Him. (Isaiah 54:13) Who are these ones? Jesus gave one way of identifying them, saying: "By this all will know that you are my disciples, if you have love among yourselves." (John 13:35) Christian love is a fruit of the spirit and a key part of the Christian new personality. Is there any group of people showing love in the way that Jesus said?

16 Well, listen to this extract from a letter written to the *New Haven Register,* a North American newspaper: "Whether you have been aggravated or ired [angered], as I have, by their proselytizing, you have to admire their dedication, their wholesomeness, their outstanding example of human behavior and healthful living." The German newspaper *Münchner Merkur* was speaking of the same group

---

16, 17. Quote some newspaper comments that help to identify those who are "taught by Jehovah" and who enjoy 'abundant peace.'

when it said: "They are the most honest and the most punctual tax payers in the [German] Federal Republic. Their obedience to the laws can be seen in the way they drive as well as in crime statistics."

17 About whom were these two newspapers talking? The same group that was discussed in the *Herald* of Buenos Aires, Argentina. This newspaper said: "Jehovah's Witnesses have proven throughout the years to be hard-working, sober, thrifty and God-fearing citizens of the kind the nation manifestly needs." A sociological study from Zambia published in the *American Ethnologist* refers to the same group. It says: "Jehovah's Witnesses experience greater success than members of other denominations in maintaining stable marital unions."

18 The newspaper *La Stampa* in Italy was also speaking of Jehovah's Witnesses when it said: "They are the most loyal citizens anyone could wish for: they do not dodge taxes or seek to evade inconvenient laws for their own profit. The moral ideals of love for neighbor, refusal of power, non-violence and personal honesty (which for most Christians are 'Sunday rules' only good for being preached from the pulpit) enter into their 'daily' way of life."

19 A South African university professor who experienced discrimination under that country's racial laws calls Jehovah's Witnesses a "people educated by the lofty standards of the Bible to be truly 'color-blind.'" Explaining this, he added: "Here are people who see what others are inside, not just the

---

18, 19. How have Jehovah's Witnesses in Italy and in South Africa been described?

color of their skin. Jehovah's Witnesses today form the only true brotherhood of mankind."

20 These comments show that there is a body of people who have opened their hearts to the Bible and upon whom God's spirit has been active. It is worthy of note that these are the same people whom we identified earlier as obeying Jesus' command to preach the good news of the Kingdom around the world. (Matthew 24:14) Why do Jehovah's Witnesses stand out in these ways? In many respects they are no different from other people. They have the same fleshly weaknesses, the same economic problems, and the same basic needs. But as a group, they love God, take the Bible seriously, and let it exert power in their lives.

21 Millions of Jehovah's Witnesses are found in more than 200 lands. They include people of every race, language, and social standing imaginable. Yet they are a united, peaceful, international brotherhood. They are good citizens of whatever country they happen to live in, but first and foremost, they are subjects of God's Kingdom, and they are all very active in telling others the good news of that Kingdom. It is truly remarkable that in this divided, hate-filled world, a group such as Jehovah's Witnesses can even exist. The fact that they do is powerful evidence that God's spirit is still active among mankind. And it is proof that the Bible is indeed "alive and exerts power."

---

20. Why do Jehovah's Witnesses stand out as different?
21. What is proved by the fact that a people such as Jehovah's Witnesses can exist in today's hate-filled world?

Chapter 14

The Bible and You

Modern critics say that the Bible is unscientific and contradictory, that it is just a collection of myths. Jesus, on the other hand, said: "Your [God's] word is truth." (John 17:17) The evidence supports Jesus rather than the critics. The facts show that the Bible is historically truthful. Moreover, its remarkable harmony, its true prophecies, its deep wisdom, and its power for good in people's lives all demonstrate that the Bible is the written Word of God. As the apostle Paul wrote: "All Scripture is inspired of God and beneficial."—2 Timothy 3:16.

THE fact that the Bible is God's word, not man's, has profound implications. It means that God really has communicated with humans. He has answered many of our questions and has shown the solution to many of our problems. It also means that the prospects for the future described in the Bible are genuine. God's Kingdom really is ruling and in time will act to remove from this earth all injustice, oppression, and suffering.

2 Now, the question is: What will you do with this information? At the very least, the knowledge

---

1. (Include introduction.) (a) What do the facts prove about the Bible? (b) What are the implications of the fact that the Bible is the inspired Word of God?
2. The knowledge that the Bible is God's Word should move you to do what?

that the Bible is God's Word should encourage you to look into it. The psalmist promised happiness for those who do so when he wrote: "Happy is the man that has not walked in the counsel of the wicked ones . . . but his delight is in the law of Jehovah, and in his law he reads in an undertone day and night."—Psalm 1:1, 2.

Accept Help

[3] Likely, in your reading of the Bible, you will find things that you do not understand. (2 Peter 3:16) An event recorded in the Bible book of Acts shows that this should be expected. Soon after the death of Jesus, an Ethiopian was reading from the prophecies of the Bible book of Isaiah. The Christian evangelist Philip met up with the man and asked: "Do you actually know what you are reading?" The Ethiopian did not, so he invited Philip to help him understand.—Acts 8:30, 31.

[4] A lady in the United States was in a similar situation. She was a regular Bible reader, but there were many important teachings of the Bible that she had not come to understand from her own reading. It was only when she had discussions with Jehovah's Witnesses that she learned of basic Bible truths, including the importance of God's Kingdom and the many blessings that the Kingdom will bring to mankind. If you invite them to, Jehovah's Witnesses will be happy to help you too so that you can better understand what you read in the Bible.

3, 4. (a) As the Bible itself shows, what should we do when we find things in the Bible that we do not understand? (b) Who are always willing to help people understand the Bible better?

Apply the Bible's Counsel

5 We are encouraged not only to read the Bible but also to act on what we read. (Psalm 119:2) In addition, the Bible encourages: "Taste and see that Jehovah is good, O you people; happy is the able-bodied man that takes refuge in him." (Psalm 34:8) In effect, it invites us to put God to the test. Try living according to God's principles, showing that you trust God to know what is best for you. Only then will you see that this truly is the right way. Those with such trust in God are really happy.

6 Some claim that no one can live by Bible principles in this dishonest, immoral, violent world. The truth is, though, that many do. Who? A young man in Africa found a group of such ones. He wrote: "I have been observing over the past few years that here in Zimbabwe it is you people, Jehovah's Witnesses, who are really trying to follow Christ's own example . . . You are the only group, so far, that has managed to convince me of God's love and the power of His gospel, through your living and not only through speeches and writings. You are living and preaching the gospel while many, many people are preaching the gospel but not living it."

Accept Its Authority

7 The apostle Paul said that the Bible is "beneficial for teaching, for reproving, for setting things straight." (2 Timothy 3:16) Sometimes, however,

---

5. According to the Bible, what course brings happiness?

6. Is it practical to try to live up to the Bible's standards today? Explain.

7. What common practices today are contrary to what the Bible says?

what the Bible says is not popular. For example, the Bible condemns homosexual acts, but homosexuality is widely viewed as an acceptable lifestyle. (Romans 1:24-27; 1 Corinthians 6:9-11; 1 Timothy 1:9-11) The Bible also says that the life of an unborn baby is important and should not be deliberately destroyed, but about 50 million abortions are performed worldwide each year. (Exodus 21:22, 23; Psalm 36:9; 139:14-16; Jeremiah 1:5) What if we personally find it difficult to accept what the Bible says on such matters?

8 Well, Christians have learned that it is always wise to follow God's Word. Why? Because in the long run, following what the Bible says always works out best for everyone. (Proverbs 2:1-11) The fact is, humans are very limited as far as wisdom is concerned. They can rarely foresee the final consequences of their actions. The prophet Jeremiah confessed: "I well know, O Jehovah, that to earthling man his way does not belong. It does not belong to man who is walking even to direct his step."—Jeremiah 10:23.

> **We should not only read the Bible but also act on what we read**

9 We have only to look around us to see that this assessment is correct. Most of the problems afflicting the world are direct results of people's not following the counsel of God's Word. The long, troubled history of mankind has shown that humans cannot successfully decide for themselves in moral

---

8, 9. When we at first find it hard to accept some point in the Bible, what should we remember, and whose standards should we always accept?

matters. God is infinitely wiser than we are. Why not accept what he says, instead of relying on our own wisdom?—Proverbs 28:26; Jeremiah 17:9.

No One Is Perfect

10 The Bible alerts us to another area in which we need help. We all have an inherited tendency to sin. "The inclination of the heart of man is bad from his youth up." (Genesis 8:21; Romans 7:21) This problem is intensified by the fact that we live in a world that does not follow Bible principles. Hence, we need help not only to understand the Bible but also to practice the things we learn. That is why the Bible encourages us to associate with others who wish to live according to godly standards. The psalmist wrote: "I have hated the congregation of evildoers, and with the wicked ones I do not sit. . . . Among the congregated throngs I shall bless Jehovah." And another psalm says: "How good and how pleasant it is for brothers to dwell together in unity!" —Psalm 26:5, 12; 133:1.

Following what the Bible says always works out for the best

11 Associating together is an essential part of worship for Jehovah's Witnesses. They have several meetings each week, as well as periodic conventions, where they study the Bible together and discuss how its principles apply in their lives. They form a worldwide "association of brothers" in which each one is encour-

---

10, 11. (a) What facts about the way we are made and the world we live in cause problems when we try to live up to the Bible's standards? (b) What kind of association does the Bible encourage us to seek, and where can we find such association?

aged and helped to maintain these high Bible standards. (1 Peter 2:17) Why not attend one of their meetings and see how such a community can help you too?—Hebrews 10:24, 25.

Live by God's Word

[12] Hence, knowing that the Bible is God's Word brings blessings and responsibilities. We are blessed because we get guidance for our daily conduct that is not available elsewhere. Further, we learn of God's love in providing his own Son to ransom us so that we might have the hope of everlasting life. (John 3:16) We realize that Jesus is now ruling as King and soon will act to remove wickedness from the earth. And we confidently await the righteous "new heavens and a new earth" that God himself has promised.—2 Peter 3:13.

[13] Bear in mind, though, that we have the responsibility to study the Bible and take to heart what it says. God himself urges: "My son, my law do not forget, and my commandments may your heart observe." (Proverbs 3:1) Even if most view the Bible as just the word of man, we should courageously "let God be found true, though every man be found a liar." (Romans 3:4) Let God's wisdom guide your life. "Trust in Jehovah with all your heart . . . In all your ways take notice of him." (Proverbs 3:5, 6) Wisely heeding God's Word in this way will affect your life for good both now and for all eternity.

---

12. What blessings come from knowing that the Bible is God's Word?

13. What responsibilities come upon us when we accept the Bible as God's Word?

References

Listed by Chapter

Chapter 1

1. *The Bible in the Modern World,* by James Barr, 1973, p. 120.
2. *The New Encyclopædia Britannica,* 1987, Vol. 2, p. 194.
3. *The Book of Books: An Introduction,* by Solomon Goldman, 1948, p. 219.
4. *The Book of Books: An Introduction,* p. 222.
5. *Federal Register,* Vol. 48, No. 26, February 7, 1983, p. 5527.
6. *Chadman's Cyclopedia of Law,* 1912, Vol. 1, pp. 86-91.

Chapter 2

1. *Ancient Near Eastern Texts,* edited by James B. Pritchard, 1969, pp. vi, xii, xiii, xiv.
2. *The Annals,* by Tacitus, Book XV. 39, 44 (*Latin Selections,* edited by Moses Hadas and Thomas Suits, 1961, p. 227).
3. *The Cambridge History of the Bible,* edited by S. L. Greenslade, 1963, Vol. 3, p. 476.
4. *Our Bible and the Ancient Manuscripts,* by Sir Frederic Kenyon, 1958, p. 50.
5. *Our Bible and the Ancient Manuscripts,* p. 79.
6. *A Light to the Nations,* by Norman K. Gottwald, 1959, p. 40.
7. *The Dead Sea Scrolls,* by Millar Burrows, 1955, pp. 303, 304.
8. *Qumran and the History of the Biblical Text,* edited by Frank Moore Cross and Shemaryahu Talmon, 1975, pp. 276, 277.
9. *An Introduction to the Books of the Old Testament,* by W. O. E. Oesterley and Theodore H. Robinson, 1958, p. 21.
10. *Our Bible and the Ancient Manuscripts,* p. 55.

Chapter 3

1. *The Lollard Bible and Other Medieval Biblical Versions,* by Margaret Deanesly, 1920, p. 24.
2. *The Lollard Bible,* p. 227.
3. *The Lollard Bible,* pp. 30-33.
4. *The Lollard Bible,* p. 36.
5. *The Lollard Bible,* p. 48.
6. *The Lollard Bible,* pp. 295, 296.
7. *The Lollard Bible,* p. 328.
8. *The History of Christian Martyrdom,* by John Foxe, 1873, p. 130; *Casiodoro de Reina, Spanish Reformer of the Sixteenth Century,* by A. Gordon Kinder, p. 16.
9. *Who Do You Say That I Am?* by Edward J. Ciuba, 1974, p. viii.
10. *The Crusades,* by Hans Eberhard Mayer, translated by John Gillingham, 1978, p. 44.
11. *The Universal History of the World,* by Edith Firoozi and Ira N. Klein, 1966, Vol. IX, p. 732.
12. *A Brief History of Ancient, Mediæval, and Modern Peoples,* by Joel Dorman Steele and Esther Baker Steele, 1883, pp. 428, 429.
13. *The Church and Its Mission: A Shattering Critique From the Third World,* by Orlando E. Costas, 1974, p. 245.
14. *If the Churches Want World Peace,* by Norman Hill and Doniver A. Lund, 1958, p. 5.

Chapter 4

1. *The Inspiration & Accuracy of the Holy Scriptures,* by John Urquhart, 1895, pp. 254, 255; *The International Critical Commentary—A Critical and Exegetical Commentary on Genesis,* Second edition, 1976, p. xlii.
2. *Encyclopædia Britannica,* 1911, Vol. xi, pp. 580, 581.
3. *The Inspiration & Accuracy of the Holy Scriptures,* pp. 262, 263; *An Introduction to the Literature of the Old Testament,* by S. R. Driver, 1898, p. 154.
4. *Who Wrote the Bible?* by Richard Elliott Friedman, 1987, p. 52.
5. *Encyclopædia Judaica,* 1971, Vol. 13, p. 264.
6. *A Survey of Old Testament Introduction,* by Gleason L. Archer, Jr., 1974, p. 107.
7. *The Inspiration & Accuracy of the Holy Scriptures,* pp. 258, 259.
8. *Ancient Near Eastern Texts,* edited by James B. Pritchard, 1969, p. 313.
9. *Biblical Archaeology Review,* May/June 1985, pp. 74, 75, 77.
10. *Archaeology of the Bible: Book by Book,* by Gaalyah Cornfeld, 1976, p. 99.
11. *The Bible and Recent Archaeology,* by Kathleen M. Kenyon, 1978, p. 97.
12. *Archaeology of the Bible: Book by Book,* p. 177.
13. *Archaeology of the Bible: Book by Book,* p. 177.
14. *The Bible in Modern Scholarship,* edited by J. Philip Hyatt, 1956, p. 297.
15. *The Story of Jericho,* by John Garstang, 1948, pp. 135, 141, 146, 186.
16. *The Illustrated Bible Dictionary,* 1980, Part 2, pp. 749, 750; *Archaeological Discoveries in the Holy Land,* 1967, p. 28.
17. *Biblical Archaeology Review,* January/February 1988, p. 54.
18. *The Land of the Bible—A Historical Geography,* by Yohanan Aharoni, 1979, p. 98.
19. *The Land of the Bible,* p. 98.
20. *The World of the Old Testament,* edited by James I. Packer, Merrill C. Tenney, and William White, Jr., 1982, p. 69.
21. *Redating the Exodus and Conquest,* by John J. Bimson, 1981, pp. 22-27, 110-115, 132-137; *Biblical Archaeology Review,* September/October 1987, pp. 45, 46.
22. *History, Archaeology, and Christian Humanism,* by William Foxwell Albright, 1964, pp. 294-296.
23. *History, Archaeology, and Christian Humanism,* pp. 294-296.

Chapter 5

1. *The Quest of the Historical Jesus,* by Albert Schweitzer, 1968, pp. 174, 186, 226.
2. *The Quest of the Historical Jesus,* p. 157; *Finding the Historical Jesus,* by James Peter, 1965, p. 24; *The Nineteenth Century in Europe—The Protestant and Eastern Churches,* by Kenneth Scott Latourette, 1959, p. 51.
3. *The Anchor Bible, The Gospel According to John,* Introduction, translation, and notes by Raymond E. Brown, 1966, Vol. 29, pp. XXI, XXII.
4. *Jesus—An Historian's Review of the Gospels,* by Michael Grant, 1977, p. 180.
5. *From the Stone Age to Christianity,* by William Foxwell Albright, 1957, pp. 383, 387; *The Anchor Bible, Mark—A New Translation With Introduction and Commentary,* by C. S. Mann, 1986, Vol. 27, p. 76.
6. *Ancient Evidence for the Life of Jesus,* by Gary R. Habermas, 1984, p. 40.
7. *Where Is History Going?* by John Warwick Montgomery, 1969, p. 51.
8. *The Text of the New Testament,* by Kurt Aland and Barbara Aland, 1987, p. 81.
9. *The Text of the New Testament,* p. 181.
10. *Jewish Antiquities,* by Josephus, Book XVIII. 116 (Loeb edition, 1969, Vol. IX, p. 81).
11. *Jewish Antiquities,* Book XX. 200 (pp. 495, 497).

12. *The Annals,* by Tacitus, Book XV. 44 (Loeb edition, 1981, Vol. V, p. 283).
13. *The Lives of the Caesars,* by Suetonius, Book V, chap. XXV (Loeb edition, 1924, Vol. 2, p. 53).
14. *The First Apology of Justin,* by Justin Martyr (published in *The Ante-Nicene Fathers,* edited by Alexander Roberts and James Donaldson, Vol. 1, p. 175).
15. *The Ante-Nicene Fathers,* Vol. 1, p. 179.
16. *Biblical Archaeological Review,* May/June 1982, pp. 30, 31.
17. *The New International Dictionary of Biblical Archaeology,* 1983, p. 294.
18. *Biblical Archaeology,* by G. Ernest Wright, 1957, p. 249.
19. *Jesus—An Historian's Review of the Gospels,* pp. 199, 200.
20. *Jesus—An Historian's Review of the Gospels,* p. 203.
21. *The International Critical Commentary—A Critical and Exegetical Commentary on the Gospel According to St. Mark,* by Ezra P. Gould, 1975, p. xliii.
22. *The Quest of the Historical Jesus,* p. 52.
23. *Living in the Shadow of the Second Coming,* by Timothy P. Weber, 1979, pp. 36, 37.

Chapter 6

1. *An Enquiry Concerning Human Understanding,* by David Hume, Sect. X, *Of Miracles* (published in *Great Books of the Western World,* 1952, Vol. 35, pp. 488-497).
2. *Discover,* November 1986, p. 34.
3. *Einstein's Universe,* by Nigel Calder, 1979, p. 40.
4. *Discover,* February 1987, p. 67.
5. *Discover,* February 1987, p. 70.
6. *Healing: A Doctor in Search of a Miracle,* by Dr. William A. Nolan, 1974, pp. 88, 89, 218, 219, 230, 231.
7. *Dialogue With Trypho,* by Justin Martyr, chap. CVIII (published in *The Ante-Nicene Fathers,* Vol. 1, p. 253).
8. *The Bearing of Recent Discovery on the Trustworthiness of the New Testament,* by Sir W. M. Ramsay, 1915, p. 222.
9. *According to Luke—A new exposition of the Third Gospel,* by David Gooding, 1987, p. 15.

Chapter 8

1. *Compton's Encyclopedia,* 1987, Vol. 7, p. 13.
2. *The Book of Popular Science* (Grolier, Inc.), 1967, pp. 213, 214.
3. *God and the Astronomers,* by Robert Jastrow, 1978, p. 14.
4. *Disturbing the Universe,* by Freeman Dyson, 1979, pp. 250, 251.
5. *Medical World News,* October 10, 1983, p. 71.
6. *New Catholic Encyclopedia,* Vol. 6, 1967, p. 252.
7. *The Neck of the Giraffe,* by Francis Hitching, 1982, p. 19.
8. *The Neck of the Giraffe,* p. 61.
9. *The World Book Encyclopedia,* 1987, Vol. 12, p. 245.
10. *Evolution: A Theory in Crisis,* by Michael Denton, 1986, pp. 249, 250.
11. *The Neck of the Giraffe,* p. 137.
12. *Evolution: A Theory in Crisis,* p. 355.
13. *Evolution: A Theory in Crisis,* p. 75.
14. *The New Encyclopædia Britannica,* 1987, Vol. 25, p. 124.
15. *Wonders of Nature,* edited by Claus Jürgen Frank, 1980, p. 87.
16. *The New Encyclopædia Britannica,* 1987, Vol. 9, p. 505.
17. *Planet Earth—Glacier,* by Ronald H. Bailey, 1982, p. 7.
18. *Scientific American,* May 1960, p. 71.
19. *Planet Earth—Ice Ages,* by Windsor Chorlton, 1983, pp. 54, 55, 57.
20. *Biblical Archaeologist,* December 1977, p. 134.
21. *The Genesis Flood,* by John C. Whitcomb, Jr. and Henry M. Morris, 1967, p. xvii.

Chapter 9

1. *The Archaeological Encyclopedia of the Holy Land,* Revised edition, edited by Avraham Negev, 1986, p. 199.
2. *The Bible After Twenty Years of Archaeology (1932-1952),* by William Foxwell Albright, 1954, p. 546.
3. *Lands of the Bible,* by J. W. McGarvey, 1880, p. 529.
4. *The History of Herodotus,* Book I. 191, Vol. 6 (published in *Great Books of the Western World,* 1952, p. 43).
5. *Nabonidus and Belshazzar,* by Raymond Philip Dougherty, 1929, p. 179.
6. *Ancient Near Eastern Texts,* edited by James B. Pritchard, 1969, p. 306.
7. *Pocket History of the World,* by H. G. Wells, 1943, p. 149.
8. *The Encyclopedia Americana,* 1977 edition, Vol. 8, p. 482.
9. *The International Critical Commentary—A Critical and Exegetical Commentary on the Book of Daniel,* by James A. Montgomery, p. 3.
10. *The Biblical Archaeologist Reader,* edited by Edward F. Campbell, Jr., and David Noel Freedman, Vol. III, 1970, p. 242.
11. *Nabonidus and Belshazzar,* pp. 183-185.

Chapter 10

1. *World Military and Social Expenditures 1987-88,* by Ruth Leger Sivard, p. 28.
2. *UN Chronicle,* June 1988, p. 18.
3. *Ending Hunger: An Idea Whose Time Has Come,* The Hunger Project edition, 1985, p. 11.
4. *Ending Hunger,* p. 7.
5. *Earthquakes: Observation, Theory and Interpretation,* Proceedings of the International School of Physics, "Enrico Fermi," 1983, p. 598.
6. *Earthquakes,* p. 603; *The New York Times,* December 30, 1988, p. A6.
7. *The World Book Encyclopedia,* 1984, Vol. 10, p. 207.
8. *World Health,* May 1988, p. 9.
9. *World Health,* July 1988, p. 8; *The German Tribune,* November 13, 1988, p. 12.
10. *World Health,* November 1986, p. 6.
11. *The Medical Post,* February 2, 1988, p. 13.

Chapter 12

1. *The Boston Globe,* February 25, 1987, p. 34.
2. *Changing Times,* July 1986, p. 26.
3. *The Times* (London), December 14, 1987, p. 12.
4. *American Journal of Psychiatry,* May 1988, pp. 558-561.
5. *Psychology Today,* October 1988, pp. 38, 39.
6. *Current Controversies in Marriage and Family,* edited by Harold and Margaret Feldman, 1985, p. 255.
7. *Ladies' Home Journal,* April 1987, p. 58.
8. *Current Controversies in Marriage and Family,* p. 42.